RESTORING THE MINISTRY OF THE PROPHET

Finding a Place for the New Believer

F. MICHAEL COLACUORI

WESTBOW
P R E S S®
A DIVISION OF THOMAS NELSON
& ZONDERVAN

WestBow Press books may be ordered through booksellers or by contacting:

WestBow Press
A Division of Thomas Nelson & Zondervan
1663 Liberty Drive
Bloomington, IN 47403
www.westbowpress.com
844-714-3454

Interior Graphics/Art Credit: Mike Reese

ISBN: 978-1-6642-9259-8 (sc)
ISBN: 978-1-6642-9258-1 (e)

Library of Congress Control Number: 2023903090

Print information available on the last page.

WestBow Press rev. date: 03/08/2023

CONTENTS

PREFACE

At some point, nearly every new Christian begins a search for his place of ministry within the body of Christ. When that begins, he is often looking far ahead to what might be his ultimate place of service. We are anxious people.

God will usually lead us through a growth process that may involve us in a series of ministries and our ultimate place of service may be reached late in life. The earlier periods may leave us with questions. What was that all about? Only in retrospect do we realize that God has had His hand on our lives for the entire time. He has been actively leading us through His plan for our lives that He had started us down long before we even became aware of it.

As we grow in the Lord, we may find ourselves looking well into the future when God is actually dealing with us today. He will use us at each and every stage of our lives, but sometimes we fail to see what is taking place. "Where are You, God? What am I supposed to be doing right now? We may be looking for both long-term and short-term answers at the same time. God will move us along at a slower rate, one that we can manage. He may not move us from A to Z all at once.

There are ways we can prepare ourselves for whatever God has for us all along the way. This book (I refer to it as a training manual) will offer suggestions that will be helpful to us no matter where we find ourselves or where we end up.

I will be offering possibilities about why the ministry of the prophet does not seem to be widely present in our generation and how it can and should be reestablished. I believe there is still a need for that ministry.

At the same time, I hope to offer ideas to those who are going through the initial portion of their Christian growth. How do we find our place of ministry? While I have written this in such a way that it might target young believers, all of us go through that process and anyone looking for his place may find it helpful.

It seems that those struggling to find their place do not always have a proactive approach. Many Christians progress through their entire lives and never lead anyone to the Lord. We can do better. It seems we sometimes become embroiled in the necessary social aspects of the church and believe that those are where we are to find our place. Those might be something that is needed by the church, but I don't believe they can replace a powerful place of ministry to fellow Christians or to unbelievers that is actually obtainable.

Not everyone will find his place as a prophet of God, but He has a place of significant ministry, *real* ministry, for all of us, and I believe this little book can help us find that place.

Chapter 1

THE MISSING MINISTRY
OF THE PROPHET

The ministry of the prophet is unique. While God had established five forms of ministry, the ministry of the prophet was quite different from the rest and fell to a very different type of person. As different as it was, ultimately, it was a very necessary ministry.

> *And he gave the apostles, the prophets, the evangelists, the pastors and teachers, to equip the saints for the work of ministry, for building up the body of Christ.* (Ephesians 4:11–12 ESV)

Each of the five had been given for the same purpose: "to equip the saints for the work of the ministry." Five ministries had originally been given, as several ways to "equip" people were necessary.

Four tended to approach their ministry by encouraging or lifting up those who were sitting under the ministry. It was a positive approach. They were telling people what they were to do. The ministry of the prophet was different. The prophet seemed to appear only when a hard and corrective voice was needed. God was telling people what not to do or where they had gone amuck.

Four ministries were leading us along from the front, while one was pushing from behind. There was a push/pull approach, and both were needed. God would first tell His people how they were to live or how to have good relationships. If they were obedient, all went well. However, there were failures. Sometimes His people were disobedient. That was when the prophet would show up.

It became his responsibility to point out, in no uncertain terms, the disobedience that had taken place and to lay out the consequences. It was a hard word delivered by men who had been raised up for just such moments. They were the corrective voice.

While it may be easy to tell people that they are doing well, to tell them that they have done poorly can be more difficult. That can actually raise up a wall between people, and the Bible tells us, "Let there be no divisions between us." Bringing a hard word may tend to keep the one bringing that word apart from the recipient. We probably don't want to hear it. Nevertheless, bringing a hard word may sometimes be necessary, even though it becomes difficult to maintain an ongoing relation with the person to whom it was given. The prophet would deliver his word and then was gone.

The prophet understood that and was often found to be living in isolation, apart from the rest of the God's people. His life became quite different from that of everyone else. Not only was his ministry unique but so was his lifestyle. It was probably a lifestyle that most of us would not choose. Perhaps it was a difficult lifestyle.

Today we seldom hear from a prophet. Is it any wonder? Who would want such a job? We seem to have lost that form of ministry, and it is my contention that we have not lost the need for it; we have only lost those who are willing to deliver such a difficult word.

Of the five, prophets are seldom heard from. If one were to be found, he would most likely speak a forceful word from God, and I am thinking that few and far between are those who are willing to put their reputation—in fact, possibly their very lives—on the line and speak out as God's own voice. I can easily understand that reluctance. It is a difficult ministry. Do prophets continue to exist, or have they gone the way of the dinosaurs? Perhaps the church can function just fine with no dinosaurs, but I am not so sure about prophets.

Each of the five ministries described in Ephesians carried out a specific and important task necessary to allow the church to function as God had designed. Throughout our Bible, we find God using each of the five ministries that He initially established, and the church was functioning well with each performing its assigned duties.

Today, it seems that only four continue to function. The ministry of the prophet is not frequently seen in operation. If it had been a necessary part of the church at first, why do we not find it functioning today? What has changed?

The very different lifestyle of the prophet might actually provide us with a hint of what has changed. People probably do not relish the rejection experienced by bringing the hard word or living in isolation. While we do have our recluses today, we do not seem to have any of them stepping forward to deal with problem situations.

We are not short on people who find themselves unable to remain close to God. That is the case today and has also been the case for each and every generation. In the past, God has used the prophet to speak directly to those who have lost their direction and to restore them. In some cases, the prophet would be called on to deliver a rejection by God.

Today we seldom see that forceful ministry taking place, and to look closely at that situation will be the subject of this manual. I believe we are still in need of that type of ministry, and it can and should be restored. Let's take a look at how it can be done.

The order in which these five ministries are presented is interesting. Apostles were the original group first trained by Jesus Himself. As time passed, they became the leadership of the entire church family. Today an apostle tends to be an overseer of many churches or a denomination. Evangelists most often cover a large area, a region, and may visit many churches, staying with each for a limited time, perhaps only three or four days. A pastor is usually the head of a single church that may be serving a community, a more localized ministry.

When we think of a teacher, often we encounter a person who is dealing with a limited number of students in one place, a decidedly localized ministry. In a Sunday school program, there might be several teachers functioning within an individual church. While there are teachers who have a far wider outreach, the more common case is that they are teaching a small group within an individual church.

The sequence presented in Ephesians seems to be given starting with the most far-reaching and ending with the most localized. This sequence places the prophet just behind the apostle in the second spot. If this sequence is offering any thinking about the relative significance of each of the five, the prophet is second only to the apostles. If so, why is it missing when the more localized three are not?

I believe the ministry of the prophet is largely missing from the church, and it is to our detriment. Therefore, the purpose of this manual will be to show that

- the office of prophet is no longer a functioning ministry
- the office remains a needed ministry of the church
- it can and should be restored
- there are steps that can be taken to restore the office of prophet to the church

A prophet would speak out as the voice of God and bring much-needed correction to the lives of those who had begun to wander off and live outside the way God had intended. Today, people continue to stray, and all five ministries had originally been given to prevent this. Why then is it *only* the office of prophet that is viewed as obsolete? Both in New Testament times and today, people fail and live in discord with the word of God. Since people continue to have problems, would that not mean that the correction brought by the prophet continues to be needed today? I believe it does.

Current leadership provides us with direct preaching of the word of God, including the benefit of obedience and the consequence of disobedience. However, I sometimes do not see that correction taking place. When people begin to stray from the Lord, seldom is there direct confrontation of the situation. Is correction not a part of the council of God? Where is the corrective voice of God? Where is a word of correction when it is called for?

Perhaps the voice of the prophet is missing not because it is unnecessary but because we have lost the understanding of how one might rise to the office and function as a prophet. How to rise to that level does not seem to be taught in Bible college and is not offered as a ministry option for students. How might students select it as their choice if the option is not presented?

Neither delivering a hard word nor living in isolation is taught in Bible college. "Delivering a Hard Word 101" is not found in the college catalog. Nor is "How to Live in a Cave 102." Or how about "How to Train Ravens to Bring Your Food 201"? God has raised up His prophets individually, providing the specialized training in unique ways.

In the days of Elisha, there were special schools just for prophets, while today our Bible colleges do not normally offer that ministry as an option. Today our young people may feel called to the ministry but are uncertain just where they might best be used. The prophetical ministry seems to have been a little different. In biblical times, those called to that ministry seem to have been immediately aware of exactly the nature of their calling and instantly began to undergo training specifically for that form of ministry.

I believe that the prophetical ministry can be restored today. I also think this can be done without restructuring our entire system of training our young people. Training received in a Bible college can be an important part of the training needed to become a prophet. Since prophets seem to live somewhat in isolation, much of their training might also be received in somewhat of an isolated situation, not in the normal Bible college environment. This may be seen as somewhat of a deviation from the way we customarily train our young people. Since our culture is not identical to that of the ancient Hebrews, some deviation might be expected.

Those who are convinced that a college degree is necessary to minister anywhere will almost certainly have difficulty with this. But God does not always do things in a manner accepted by society or even by the church. No two prophets may have received the exact same training, and the training they *did* receive may have begun well before they even understood the plan of God for their lives.

While in Elisha's day there had been schools for prophets, we do not really know if any of its graduates were ever used to the extent we have seen God use the major prophets (big Old Testament books). Perhaps they were all individually trained by God Himself. While each brought the word of God, each seems to be a specific ministry brought about to meet the needs of a specific time.

Those who are leaders of Bible colleges today may not easily warm up to the idea that a prophet cannot be adequately trained by conventional methods. This is not intended to be a criticism of the important role played by those schools in the development of our young people. We need more, not fewer, of them to attend our Bible colleges. The case I am making is that the roll of the prophet is a special ministry for special situations and requires training not readily available through conventional methods. We will shortly see how this takes place.

Some may be prone to feel that the pastor is fulfilling the function of the prophet by "speaking forth" the word of God. Indeed, pastors do that every Sunday. However, I do not feel that what a pastor speaks is quite the same thing as what a prophet does.

The pastor can offer his interpretation of God's word, may do so forcefully, and can offer encouragement and in-depth teaching as well. That's quite a lot of responsibility for one person to assume. In spite of the heavy load borne by the pastor, it may not end there. In many churches, the pastor also tackles the management aspects of holding a church together. However, there is a limit. He is still only one person and is busy enough without taking on the additional responsibilities of the prophet. He needs to maintain an ongoing relationship with his flock and normally doesn't feel that he can risk breaking it.

The prophet confronts the more difficult situations directly and brings a hard word that is sometimes not well received. He speaks directly to specific ways in which someone has broken with God's leading. For a pastor to also take on that responsibility might put a strain on his relationship with his flock.

There are those who feel that the written word, the Bible, has replaced some things that were originally dealt with by men of God. To believe that the written word can replace the confrontative word brought by a prophet is a stretch. To receive correction from the written word, the Bible must be opened and read. An individual must turn to his Bible voluntarily. It will bring correction *only* if it is opened and read. When people have begun to stray, the time that correction is most needed, is the time when their Bible is least likely to be opened. I believe that God understands this and has provided a means to bring about correction when none is sought.

Even among those who know their Bible well, if they begin to stray, their knowledge of God's word that reminds them they are moving away from God may not help. They will not only avoid Bible reading as they move away from God, but they will probably close their minds to what had already been implanted into their spirit. They will no longer want to be reminded of the truth that it contains. In effect, they may attempt to hide from God.

The prophet approaches a person when correction is needed, whether the one who has slipped is seeking help or not. It is an intervention of mercy. Where is this merciful intervention today? As long as people stray from God, the office of prophet will continue to be needed. My belief is that it remains a needed position of the church and effort should be undertaken to reestablish it.

King Saul, through the prophet Nathan, had been instructed to wipe out the Amalekites. Saul was not fully compliant and God rejected him from being king over Israel because of his failure. These are his words delivering the news to the rebellious Saul:

> *Because you have rejected the word of the Lord, he has rejected you from being king.*
> (1 Samuel 15:23)

Where do we have a pastor who can openly confront our political leadership and prophecy his removal from his office *and have it come to pass?* We don't. This type of confrontation is completely foreign to our church today and would be outside the duties of a pastor. Only a true prophet is capable of this type of word.

The history of our nation clearly shows the unmistakable hand of God throughout. However, today many do not seem to believe that the leadership of our nation has been established or even blessed by God. For many, the opinion of how government is created has changed. Viewing our secular leadership as having been established independently from God leaves God with no apparent authority over our leadership.

Today's political leadership is unlikely to listen to someone confronting him with a word of warning. The prophet would probably be arrested and accused of "hate crimes." However, lack of recognition by the leadership would not stop a true prophet from speaking out. If God wants to be heard, He will raise up His voice irrespective of the circumstances.

Our pastors can spearhead the restoration of a major prayer effort to bring about a change in attitude about this, but at this moment, they would be completely unable to take an effective public stand against the actions of our government. The church is not yet ready to take up this challenge. The function of the pastor is to lead that change in attitude. He should prepare his congregation to face ungodly leadership. That alone is a challenge large enough for the office of pastor.

A prophet will often appear on the horizon when things are at their very worst. Today many do not see the influence of God as crucial. Before a prophet could confront leadership directly, a series of disasters would probably proceed a direct confrontation from a prophet. The nation would most likely be broken and in desperate straits. Voters would have to be ready to look beyond secular leadership for answers.

The leadership decisions being made in early 2021 could be the beginnings of bad decisions that may lead to that desperation. Those decisions may bring about the appearance of a prophet with a major ultimatum. Perhaps the church would not be involved in raising up such a prophet at all. If he is raised up directly by God, he could appear unexpectedly, fully trained, and ready to speak out. His ultimatum might first be directed at the church. Get it on board, with prayer first. The time could be right to see the restoration of the prophetical ministry.

The captivity of the Hebrews in Egypt was of a spiritual nature. During their time in Egypt, the Hebrews had been well fed and seemed to enjoy life. Where was their cry for deliverance? In the natural, they were satisfied. Most of us have been taught that their plea was for physical deliverance. However, it was not as we are usually taught. Things were going well.

> *And the whole congregation grumbled against Moses and Aaron in the wilderness, and the people of Israel said to them, "Would that we have died by the hand of the Lord in the land of Egypt, **when we sat by the meat pots and ate bread to the full,** for you have brought us out into this wilderness to kill this whole assembly with hunger." (Exodus 16:2–3 ESV; emphasis mine)*

This is not the cry of a people desperate to be freed from captivity. They were happy campers in Egypt. However, their relationship with the living God was in trouble. They not only had adopted the cultural ways of Egypt, but they were also gradually adopting the worship of pagan gods. They needed to reestablish their relationship with their God, and they may have been unaware of their need to do so.

See if You Can Sort This Out

The very idea of slavery has been a somewhat difficult concept. The Bible clearly refers to the Hebrews as being in slavery in Egypt. Moses also found it necessary to ask Pharaoh for permission for his people to leave. It they were truly free, that would not seem to have been necessary. They were also living in "oppression" for a portion of that time and Pharaoh would not have pursued them if he didn't want them back. All of that smacks of literal slavery.

The scripture given above supports the idea that they were not slaves. In addition, many of those who have a very good knowledge of Egyptian history feel that there had been no slavery in Egypt (as we know it) before Roman times.

It is also clear that spiritual slavery was the most significant aspect of this issue that the Bible wants us to get a grasp of. No matter how the historical side of this plays out, we need to understand what God

was doing in their lives at the spiritual level. If you can sort this out, let me know.

The confrontation of Pharaoh by the prophet Moses appeared to have taken place at the physical level. Egypt was gradually broken and left in ruins. However, the purpose of the confrontation was to demonstrate that the living God was the real God and that the Pharaoh of Egypt was, at best, a poor substitute. Even though the visible battle was carried out at the physical level, the purpose remained spiritual. Not the Egyptians only, but the Hebrews as well needed to understand that the living God was the real God. They needed to reestablish their covenant with Him.

Today, our nation has been blessed beyond anything experienced by any other people. Physically we do not need deliverance. At the same time, for the past few decades, we have been slipping spiritually. Church attendance is down, fewer children are participating in summer camp, and we are having fewer new converts. Today, many churches have only a Sunday morning service. It is at the spiritual level that we need deliverance today.

God will use the natural world to show where we have fallen short. The physical world is the mirror image of the spiritual world. While the condition of our physical affairs may seem to be in trouble, our shortfall has taken place primarily at the spiritual level. Things that are taking place in the world today are calling attention *not* to the natural world but to the condition of things in the spiritual world.

Those who endeavor to fix the problems in the physical world have their hearts in the right place, but their effort will probably not produce the desired result. This is the time to return to God. If we restore our relationship with Him, only then will we see things begin to change in the visible world that we so desperately want to see.

Does that seem backward to you? It's not. What is taking place in the physical world is the mirror image God is providing of our spiritual condition. There is a purpose for our physical situation. It is to call our attention to our spiritual plight. God's effort is focused primarily on the spiritual.

As a nation, the opinion that political leadership is given by God will have to again become the norm before a challenge from a prophet to the secular government can be successfully made. Only when the attitude of the country is due for change will a prophet appear and stand against the leadership. He will probably appear when things seem to be at their very worse.

Even a prophet will be in need of prayer support to raise the challenge that will be needed. The prophet is the voice of God. Only when the church is ready for a change will his voice also become the voice of the church. Change must come to the church first and that will require a change to the individual. The ballot box will then follow.

The change at the physical level will be the reflection of what has taken place in the spiritual arena. The route to restoring the economic well-being of our nation is the restoration of our walk with God. We are blessed when we are obedient.

After David had taken Bathsheba, the wife of Uriah the Hittite, the prophet Nathan confronted David using an allegory about a rich man with many sheep who had taken the only sheep of a poor man. After David denounced this man, Nathan said, "Thou art the man" (2 Samuel 12:7 KJV)! Notice that it was *the prophet,* not a priest, who confronted David.

It would be difficult for a pastor to confront someone so directly and continue with the same relationship he would normally maintain with his flock. The pastor is charged with holding his congregation together. This confrontation is the responsibility of the prophet. He is an outsider and can more readily speak a harsh word. It's hard to be an insider and an outsider at the same time. Keeping these two ministries separate makes for a better division of leadership.

If those who want to combine the ministries of pastor with teacher also want to fold the prophet into the same office, they are reducing the fivefold ministry from five to three, placing an even greater burden on the pastor. It's OK. Pastors don't need a day off anyway. They can work twenty-four/seven, right? *Wrong!* That much responsibility is too great for a single individual. All three continue to be needed as separate ministries.

Is This for Me?

Since we have few, if any, people functioning as prophets, God will have to raise up new men of God. Are you interested? It would be an important ministry and is badly needed. If it sounds good, read on.

Chapter 2

THE WAY IT WAS

When the servant of the man of God rose early in the morning and went out, behold,
an army with horses and chariots was all around the city. And the servant said, "Alas,
my master! What shall we do?" He said, "Do not be afraid, for those who are with us
are more than those who are with them." Then Elisha prayed and said, "O Lord, please
open his eyes that he may see. So the lord opened the eyes of the young man, and he saw,
and behold, the mountain was full of horses and chariots of fire all around Elisha."
—2 Kings 6:15–17 (ESV)

A Prophet and His Student

There were more with Elisha than with the enemy. However, notice the phrase "than those who are with them." The enemy was not entirely alone either. Both sides had spirit beings that accompanied them. While the battle would have been physical, if it had taken place, the good guys had the greater number of angels. Like many battles, this one would ultimately been won in the spirit. The prophet understood where the real battle was to have taken place. His student may not have understood that just yet.

Elisha did not need to see that he was surrounded with help from God. He already knew it. These two men were not functioning with the same level of spiritual discernment. Elisha knew they were there. He had discerned their presence. When he actually saw God's invisible army, he was not strengthened further because he already completely understood that God was there and was on his side. The prophet did not need to see with his eyes.

You might notice that Elisha appeared to have done nothing immediately. He almost seemed to be unconcerned about their presence. It was only when they "came down against him" that he took action. What he did shows he had already been hearing from God and understood how he was to handle it. Dealing with the situation fell to the prophet rather than the army of Israel.

He had been waiting for a word from God and did not rush it. As a result of having waited, he both knew about their presence and also what to do about it; they were two entirely different bits of information. Yet he had absolute confidence about the outcome.

What happened next is dumbfounding. The revelation that God's army was there was only the beginning. That knowledge only opened the door to understand exactly how God was going to turn the battle.

> *And when the Syrians came down against him, Elisha prayed to the Lord and said: "Please strike the people with blindness." So he struck them with blindness in accordance with the prayer of Elisha. And Elisha said to them, "This is not the way and this is not the city. Follow me and I will bring you to the man who you seek." And he led them to Samaria.* (2 Kings 6:18–19 ESV)

Whose idea had it been to strike them with blindness? Did Elisha come up with that, or had God spoken to him about what measures were to be taken. Whichever it had been, Elisha was praying "according to the will of the Father" (Romans 8:26–27). It had been the plan of God that was being initiated.

The enemy had become confused. They had come to attack Israel but calmly followed Elisha back to Samaria. Were they looking for only a man? Were they about to attack the wrong place? They could see with their eyes but had lost all awareness of where they were or why they had come. The entire army had been blinded.

They could still see to follow Elisha but were unable to understand the reasons for their assault. They had no discernment whatsoever. God had moved not only in Elisha's life but in theirs as well. Elisha not only was aware of their presence, but he also had absolute confidence that God would answer his prayer and "blind" them. Elisha had to act quickly, and he would have no time for a second chance. If God had not answered that prayer just as Elisha had asked, it would have been too late for plan B.

> *As soon as they entered Samaria, Elisha said, "O Lord, open the eyes of these men, that they may see." So the Lord opened their eyes and they saw, and behold, they were in the midst of Samaria.* (2 Kings 6:20 ESV)

They were trapped with no way out. Elisha, counter to what you might expect, did not have them killed. He held a feast, feeding the enemy and sending them on their way. No battle was fought, yet Israel was victorious. A great victory was won with no sword lifted. The Syrians understood that the God of Israel had tricked them and ensnared them in an unescapable trap. God had revealed his greatness to the Syrians!

While they had initially surrounded the army of Israel, they now found themselves surrounded by that same army! God not only knows how to handle a bad situation, but He does so in a way that makes the plans of men look foolish. We may view God as being serious at all times. While He surely is serious, I believe He also has a sense of humor! God had a far better way to deal with the Syrians than Israel, on its own, could have ever come up with. Mercy prevailed.

There was only one man who understood the ways of God well enough to be used in such an unbelievable way. Only Elisha was able to discern, not see, the presence of God's army. Even in the time of Elisha, the ability to exercise spiritual discernment to that degree wasn't widespread. It was well developed only in Elisha. Even in the days when prophets were an accepted part of the church, those able to minister at that level were few and far between.

Elisha was held in high regard. Israel's army did not panic at their presence but was willing to trust the man of God. Likewise, when they arrived at Samaria, those in the city did not panic at the arrival of the Syrians. Normally to see an army of the enemy calmly marching straight into the heart of their city would have been a huge wake-up call. The army would have been placed on full alert and become battle ready. However, everyone had complete confidence in Elisha. They seem to have remained at peace. His reputation had been well established.

For Elisha, discernment was only the beginning. Knowing the army of the Lord was there was the first step. He also understood what to do next. There might have still been a battle if Elisha had not had a further revelation of how to use the knowledge that he had been given. However, he understood that the Lord had a way to win the battle before it began. He would fool the enemy.

God had moved on behalf of Elisha four times. He had opened the eyes of Elisha's servant, He blinded the Syrians, He caused them to calmly follow Elisha back to Samaria, and finally God reopened the eyes of the Syrians. The servant was on hand to experience the entire series of events. He was learning.

A Word of Encouragement

God did not throw this servant into the fire with no help. He was sending him through a very carefully crafted training program. He would provide one for you as well. You would not be alone. Sounds good?

People who read this passage for the first time sometimes find this sequence of events amazing. They do not seem to be surprised that God would move so mightily to help His people, but that man could be so discerning to see it and know how to proceed is somewhat foreign to the church today. That He would move to confound the enemy is also unexpected. Readers often find this story absolutely incredible.

I would submit that this type of sensitivity was never intended to be unusual. God does not communicate with man vocally. That is done through the spirit, and few of us have developed the ability to communicate with God so precisely in both directions.

Most of us have confidence enough to know that when we pray, God actually hears our prayers. Why should it seem so difficult to believe that when God speaks to us that we can hear Him as well? If we fail to hear, how are we supposed to know what we are to do? It should be a two-way street. Would that not be good communication? The capacity to communicate with God at that level remains within us. However, it requires time and effort to develop.

At that early point, the young man, Elisha's servant, was unable to communicate with God at the spiritual level. He was only able to believe when he saw the enemy. He was not yet where Elisha was. However, the reason that he had become the servant of Elisha was that he was being trained.

God may have recognized that he had potential. Potential does not necessarily mean he was exceptionally intelligent. It meant he would listen and learn. He had not panicked when he saw his camp surrounded. He looked to Elisha for a solution; meanwhile, Elisha looked to God. The trainee was able to see just how God would use Elisha to resolve the conflict.

The servant was willing to learn, and he didn't attempt to do all the talking. He evidently says nothing further for the balance of the encounter. He was willing to watch and listen to his teacher and had been handpicked to sit under Elisha and learn. He did it.

At that point in his life, that was all that he could handle and no more was asked of him. A young servant is not expected to have well-developed spiritual discernment at the outset. It takes time to develop, and the young servant's discernment would grow as he watched the more spiritually mature Elisha in operation.

Drink It In

The servant didn't have to worry about how his training would progress. God had things well under control. This was OJT. He was observing what God was doing in the real world.

The Passing of the Mantle

In the beginning, Elisha would not have exercised a high level of discernment himself. It was only after he had trained under Elijah for years that the mantle passed to him from Elijah. By then, he was ready to assume the role of God's prophet. Everyone must come to maturity, and the development of spiritual discernment is an extremely important aspect of that process. The need for a prophet of God would not end with the taking up of Elijah.

On the day that the mantle was to pass, Elisha was very well aware of the big change that was about to take place and was determined to take in every scrap of information on his very last day as an understudy. He refused to leave Elijah. When the sons of the prophets said to him, *"Do you know that today the Lord will take away your master from you?"* Elisha replied, *"Yes, I know it, keep quiet"* (2 Kings 2:3).

The sons of the prophets had discerned it. Elijah had discerned it. Elisha had discerned it, and it came up twice. In saying "keep quiet," he was saying, "Go away and don't try to distract me!" He would not allow his focus on what was happening to be broken.

As the day developed, Elisha asks that a double portion of Elijah's spirit would come upon him (2 Kings 2:9). Elijah says this will only be possible if Elisha actually sees him taken up, and Elisha was not about to miss it. It would be granted if Elisha's discernment would remain unbroken.

Elijah had said, "You have asked a hard thing." It was not difficult for God to grant his request. It was difficult for Elisha to notice the very quick exit of Elijah. It would only be possible if Elisha was alert enough to see the speedy exodus that was about to take place. He understood that he would be taken up in a flash, in no time at all, and he knew how easily it could be missed. Elisha was ready for his final examination. He would settle for no less than an A+ on his report card.

Elisha's discernment was fully developed by this time, and this was the acid test. Could his focus on what was happening be broken? Could he miss God? The sons of the prophet tried to break it twice, and Elijah tested him on this point as well. The major effort that had been put into attempting to cause Elisha to lose his focus is clear evidence of the importance of maintaining focus. To hear from God, the prophet must *maintain focus.*

> *And as they still went on and talked, behold, chariots of fire and horses of fire separated the two of them. And Elijah went up by a whirlwind into heaven. And Elisha saw it and he cried "My father my father! The chariots of Israel and its horsemen!" And he saw him no more.* (2 Kings 2:11–12 ESV)

This event did not require hours. It lasted for only a brief second, and Elisha could easily have missed it if he had lost his focus even momentarily. That it appears as the cover of this manual does not mean that it was frozen in time. In the blink of an eye, it was over. Elisha would not be distracted for even a single second, and he was rewarded by seeing Elijah taken up.

After Elijah was taken up, Elisha tore his own clothes. (His past was behind, and his training was over.) He took up Elijah's cloths. (His new ministry was about to begin.) And he struck the water, saying, *"Where is the Lord, the God of Elijah?" And when he had struck the water, the water parted to the one side and to the other, and Elisha went over* (2 Kings 2:14).

Elijah had recently done the very same thing. He had struck the water, and he and Elisha had crossed over. Elisha was looking for confirmation that he was indeed now the successor to Elijah. Both partings are something of a confirmation that God recognized them each as equal to Moses, who is sometimes thought to have been the greatest of prophets.

Moses had also struck the water of the Red Sea that immediately parted, allowing the entire Hebrew nation to pass. When the Hebrews crossed the River Jordan, the waters were also parted. The parting of the waters signaled that God was with them. The past was behind. The future lay ahead. A new door of opportunity was opening. God would be with them in the future.

For Elisha, the mantle had now passed; it now rested on him. Elisha had quietly waited for God to affirm him as prophet. He did not jump the gun. He wanted solid confirmation from the Lord that he was now the prophet. He *would not* move until it came. His training would not be fully complete until he was confirmed, and he waited patiently until it came.

Even though he had seen Elijah taken up, he still looked for confirmation that he was now the prophet. His final test had been that he had to maintain focus through several major distractions. If that was his final test, it makes very good sense that these three—waiting, listening, and maintaining focus—were all important components of his many years of training.

Let's Think about It

Your training will take place as you witness what God is doing all around you. You will watch as others execute the things you will be learning, waiting, listening, and maintaining focus. After you have mastered them, you will then begin to function using those same ministry skills.

A Review of Principles Introduced by Seeing Elisha in Action

If it seems that today we are functioning without discernment, perhaps we are. We may have a lot to learn. However, I think we have covered quite a bit of ground already in this opening portion. Several important principles have already been mentioned, and I think a quick recap might be in order.

- *Communication* with God should be a two-way street.
- Learning to *listen* is a critical component of training.
- *Hearing* the word of God goes a step beyond listening.
- Elisha had been *waiting* for God to make the first move.
- He understood how to *use* the word he had received.
- *Training* is absolutely necessary.
- Maintaining *focus* is critical.
- The need for *discernment* has not been lost, and discernment remains available to those who are willing to develop it.

Chapter 3

THE WAY IT IS TODAY

Where Are Today's Prophets?

This discussion is primarily about the restoration of the prophetical ministry to the church. In that respect, prophets have to come from somewhere, and I will be offering suggestions to young Christians who may not have already found a place of ministry for themselves within the church. As a new Christian, you may have to learn much to grow to maturity. Hopefully, this manual will benefit you as you attempt to find your place within the body of Christ.

God has more for His servants than setting up tables for church potlucks. The social aspects of the church are important, and that job needs to be done, but your turn for that will not substitute for the ministry that awaits you. Today it is very rare to see someone who is hearing directly from God, seeing into people's lives, and bringing about striking changes. While we may have a few, fewer still are ever recognized as the prophet of God.

Occasionally there is someone who attempts to assume the title of prophet himself. Be careful! That is the sole responsibility of God. God calls. The individual responds. The church confirms. In his book *The Day and the Hour,* Francis Gumerlock has assembled many prophecies extending from the time of Christ to today, twenty centuries in all. Those prophecies covered only three things: the return of Jesus, the revelation of the antichrist, and the end of the world.

They totaled 960 prophecies, about one every two years for twenty centuries. *None of them have ever come to pass.* In the Bible, false prophets were stoned. None of those who made those so-called prophecies were ever stoned. Several of the self-proclaimed prophets mentioned in that book actually made more than one prophecy. When their original prophecy failed to come about, some made new a one, extending their projected date farther into the future.

While I was participating in the 1987 Christian Bookseller's Convention, there was an inordinate amount of excitement across the entire convention hall about a newly released book titled *88 Reasons Why Jesus Is Coming in 1988.* My own pastor at the time, a man who was normally extremely cautious about believing such predictions, was taken in by it. Guess who never showed up. The following year, the same author released a book entitled *89 Reasons Why Jesus Is Coming in 1989.* It garnered far less attention. If nothing else, even the author was acknowledging that Jesus had not come in 1988.

I no longer remember the name of the author of that book. His heart would seem to have been in the right place. He saw the condition of the world, knew that change was badly needed, felt that the Lord was the only answer, and was anxious to see God at work. All of that was good. However, his prophecy was not real; he jumped the gun. He had not heard from God.

God calls prophets individually. There is no line of succession. The son of a prophet does not routinely succeed his father as prophet. That is somewhat different from the way the Levitical priesthood was chosen. In that priesthood, the son often did follow the father's footsteps. Even the prophet Samuel failed to understand that. He appointed his own sons to succeed himself as prophet and they failed miserably (1 Samuel 8:1).

That had also been the case with the sons of Eli, Samuel's predecessor. Eli had appointed his sons to succeed him, and they were not men of God's choosing (1 Samuel 1:12). However, it had not been Eli who took the initial steps to raise up Samuel as the next prophet. God alone had called Samuel.

Prophets were not selected in the same way as priests. The very fact that there is no line of succession alludes to the idea that the ministry is important enough that God would individually select them and not trust it to tradition. The office was not only different from the priesthood but was also a higher calling.

In the natural world, the son often does follow his father as either the head of the family or to run the family business. However, that is not the way God's economy works. Samuel and Eli had both elevated their own sons to the office of prophet, and they were far from being God's choice.

When Israel pleaded for a king, God responded by directing Samuel to anoint Saul king. That choice had been made by the people, not God, and was based on Saul's physical stature; he was "head and shoulders" taller than other men. From a worldly perspective, Saul probably looked like a good choice. However, he had not been God's choice. God was about to give the Hebrews a taste of what they pleaded for: a worldly leader. It was not God's best and Saul ultimately was a failure as king.

The idea that prophets are chosen directly by God is important. Surely, if they were chosen by men, we would have no shortage of prophets today. Men would probably promote people from among the established priesthood, offering the best of the priests a place to move if they did well. God does not have a quota that must be filled. Those He called seemed to have been chosen long before they were even close to being ready for such a ministry. They do not seem to have been brought up through the priesthood. Their special calling was on them from the start.

Samuel, even as a prophet of God, had made the wrong call. He had not heard from God about who might succeed him, and it had been his obviously bad choice of his own sons as prophets that prompted Israel to call for a king rather than a prophet (1 Samuel 8:4–5).

Israel had specifically asked for a worldly leader. What they were asking would take them in the exact opposite direction from where God wanted them to go. They were asking amiss. God was about to give them what they had asked for: a worldly leader. They wanted man's way, not God's way. They were asking for trouble.

Samuel also nearly anointed the tallest of David's brothers to replace Saul as the next king. Picking leaders does not seem to have been his best strength. Three straight failures of the same nature might suggest something about Samuel's ability to pick leaders. He was clearly not hearing from God on leadership selection in either the spiritual or the physical areas.

Are prophets perfect people? No. Do prophets always listen for the voice of God? Not always. When Samuel selected his own sons to succeed him, he does not seem aware that he was making the selection with no word from God. When prophets listen, do they always hear? Just because a person is elevated to the office of prophet, it does not make him immune to failure. Samuel had lost his focus.

Saul remained king until his own death, and Samuel was not removed as prophet because he had made mistakes. "The gifts and calling of god are without repentance" (Romans 11:29). Both men held their positions until their deaths. Even in the face of failure, God did not quickly replace them. A board of directors might have reconsidered their decision when they saw the failure of their chosen leader.

No Worries!

If you are chosen by God, you will never have to fear that you are only as good as your last decision. If you are repentant when you blow it, God will continue to use you and provide additional enlightenment all along the way.

To continue to hear from God, a prophet must retain focus each and every day and at each and every moment. Maintaining focus is not easy. Distractions are many, and a person, even a prophet, can easily drop his guard. If you were called to be a prophet, could you keep your guard up at all times? It can be done, but this situation may demonstrate why training is long and arduous.

There is nothing wrong with having people nearby who also hear from God and who are able to confirm a word. The prophet is not the only servant who is called to hear the voice of God. The strength of the church is at its best when we have layers of discerning leadership.

Not only prophets, but all of God's servants are called individually. Nobody automatically rises to the position of his predecessor. Every person, every generation, and every prophet must learn how to follow God, and it is difficult enough with God as the teacher. With man as the teacher, it is doomed to failure.

Scripturally, the acid test to determine if a prophecy was from God was to have been whether the prophecy actually came to pass. If it did not, it was not from God (Deuteronomy 18:22)! While we need the ministry of prophets today, we need to be very careful in accepting anyone as a prophet, especially if he makes the claim himself.

Elisha did not declare himself to be the prophet after picking up Elijah's cloths. Only when the waters parted, when God had performed a miracle at Elisha's own hand, when he had received confirmation from God, did he begin to minister as a prophet. That first miracle was specifically for Elisha. The waters parted not so much that Elisha could cross but so Elisha would experience the confirmation of himself as the prophet. It was a symbolic crossing.

Many believe that God no longer deals with people through prophets, and the very lack of seeing them in action may further cause people to believe that such ministry is no longer possible. Some believe that once the Bible had been given to us, the written word is all that is necessary and we can depend on that alone to carry us through with no prophet speaking out as the voice of God.

I am in *partial* agreement with that line of reasoning. The word of God is now at our fingertips and we can devour it at any time. It has become our ultimate message from God. However I do not feel that his written word is the *only* platform through which God speaks. He continues to use people.

A Thought for the Thinker

> **Are you a people? If so, you may be God's chosen vessel to proclaim His word. God wants to use you to reach others. God is willing to use you. Are you up for this? God thinks you are.**

There seems to be something about a written page that tends to garner the greatest confidence in the accuracy of the message. The old adage "Seeing is believing" may come into play here. The very declaration that the Bible is our final word from God actually somewhat closes the door on anyone ministering as a prophet today.

Reading and studying the Bible may actually become factors that limit our ability to hear directly from God. Concentrating our effort on studying God's written word means that we are putting less, if any, effort into hearing directly from God in any other way. If we have not developed the ability to hear God's voice, we will not hear directly from Him. The Bible was never intended to be a limitation on how we might hear from God. It was to be a foundation against which everything we might receive from God was to have been measured.

If we expect to find God *only* in His written word, we will not be expecting to hear from Him in any other way. If we are not, we will surely lower our spiritual antennas and we will miss Him when he shows up. When the Old Testament prophets were ministering to God's people, the written word had either not come into use yet, or it was relatively new. The proto-Hebrew language seems to have appeared around 1500 BC. However, God has not changed. He is still out there, and He is much easier to touch than we sometimes anticipate today. He is only a prayer away.

In the days of Samuel and Elijah, there were schools for the prophets (2 Kings 2:3). The need for training up and coming prophets was recognized even then, during the day when the prophet was an accepted part of experiencing God. What has changed? Are we not in need of people who are in very close contact with God? Are those who have a greater ability to reach out and touch God not helpful to us today?

We expect our pastors to have a word from God, and they do. However, a prophet may have a word from God that potentially is of a different sort from what our pastors have received. It tends to be a hard word delivered at a time when the recipient is not willing to accept something less forceful. What's so difficult to believe about that? Both had been given as different ministries. I believe the ministry of the prophet is still needed and can be reestablished.

The Bible teaches us principles by which we can order our lives, and I am not proposing that we alter that. However, there are times when principles will not speak specifically enough to us and a special word directly from God is in order. That is not to say that any word can be in opposition to what He has already put into His word. All prophecy must align itself with the written word.

I am not attempting to diminish the importance of God's word. However, I do believe that it is possible to communicate directly with God with no published communication as the vehicle. The Bible is only one way, albeit an important way, that God can communicate with us. Not prophets only, but average believers can and should develop discernment well enough to hear from God directly.

God has created us to function best when we are interacting with others. He made us to be "people people." The faith of others rubs off on us, and it rises to a higher level when we witness the faith of someone else in action followed by a direct response from God. We benefit from hearing directly from other believers what God has done for them. What He has done for others, He will do for us.

What Does a Prophet Actually Do?

The testimony of the family of God shows us what God can do for us. The prophet drives home the point as to how we are to conduct ourselves. God will intervene at the most difficult of moments. This can best take place when we are able to experience a man of God ministering to our spiritual needs.

The job description of a prophet is very simple. He listens. He hears. He speaks. As simple as it sounds, it's a difficult job. The learning process will move him through the listening and into the hearing mode. We will have covered that progression in other places, and I won't go into it further here. Suffice to say, most will find it necessary to slow way down, listen carefully, and say very little in order to grasp what God is saying. To first recognize the voice of God and then understand exactly what He is saying will probably require more concentration than you might have expected.

It might seem that once you have received a word from God, the rest is easy. All you have to do is pass it along to those for whom is was given. It's easy, right? Many of the words you will receive as a prophet will be given to point out the error of those to whom it is given. They probably ain't gonna like it.

Have you ever heard a prophecy telling how wonderfully someone has done? I doubt it. You will be delivering a badly needed message demanding immediate change with severe consequences for failure. You will often be delivering a hard message to an unreceptive audience who may very well view you as the problem, "you troubler of Israel" (1 Kings 18:17)!

When the Going Gets Tough?

God's prophets were tough, but they may not have started out that way. It was part of their training. They toughened up. Where do you stand on that. How tough are you? You may need to toughen up as well. Is this enough to get you to quit? No? Good. It never stopped Elijah either.

A prophet is normally not in daily contact with a specific congregation. Some prophets are a little reclusive. Being somewhat separate on a daily basis can make him a better voice to bring a difficult word to a person or persons. The very fact that he has *not* been in recent contact with those to whom he ministers makes it easier for witnesses to understand that his revelations have come from God. He would not have known the needs of people with whom he was not associated. (Not unless he had been hearing from God!)

The daily, ongoing responsibility of a local pastor to his own congregation places him in a position where he may not be the best person to bring forth a hard word. The voice of the pastor is primarily heard within the church while that of the prophet may be heard beyond its walls.

Today each community has many churches. While most of us have placed our membership with a local body, there is really very little that requires us to stay with that particular group. At the first sign of conflict, anyone who chooses can move to another church and will most likely be welcomed with open arms.

This places a pastor in a somewhat precarious position. If he is too accommodating with his people, he will weaken his ability to impart the more difficult teachings from the word. On the other hand, if he is too forceful, he may drive off those to whom he is called to minister. The more forceful word might better come from an outsider, the prophet.

Those who are in need of correction may not want to hear the word you will have for them, and you may be blamed for the word itself. They may be mad at you, not at God. You may take the brunt of their outrage when they hear what you have to say. Prophets do not show up as cheerleaders.

If your own nature is to kick back and relax, delivering a forceful word may go against your nature. Be prepared to undergo change in your very nature during your training. You may have to learn to speak out when you might have wanted to take a back seat. Step up. Speak out.

On the other hand, what if your nature is to quickly step up and deliver a forceful message for immediate change? Would you too quickly step out on your own without hearing from God? That may also require something of a change. Listen quick. Speak slow.

That is not to say that your personality needs to change. You may have noticed that the personalities of Elijah and Elisha were entirely different. While Elijah and been a rougher outspoken individual, Elisha was more settled and polite.

God does not select His servants because of their personality. He chooses the willing and uses people of widely different personalities, even to the extent that the one who directly followed Elijah was very different from who he had been. God did not want to duplicate Elijah. He wanted to duplicate His message to His people.

If They Did It, You Can Do It

You are your own person. You do not have to duplicate your predecessor. God has accepted you the way you are. Your own personality has been implanted within you by God. He is satisfied with his creation. You can be too.

Will you be reluctant to pass along a hard word? Will you look for a way to soften the blow? Did God give it to you only to have you to water it down, or did He want it delivered the way in which it was given to you? Why did he give you the message? A word cannot be looked upon as loving if it weakens the blow and fails to deal with a situation badly needing change. People will not change until they understand how far out of line they have gotten, and prophets do not normally speak against minor issues. The job of the prophet is usually to speak forth a word that is difficult for the receiver to hear.

The difference in the delivery between the pastor and the prophet is significant. A pastor will speak out a word, even forcefully, but that is normally a word of enlightenment or encouragement. The prophet will speak out a word, even forcefully, that is often an ultimatum. Failure to comply will result in judgment coming to the recipient.

How Do You Become a Prophet?

There are no help-wanted signs out for this job. The pay is low. (You may be eating locusts and wild honey for dinner, per Matthew 3:4–6.) Would you like to have your food brought to you? Possibly so, but would it look appetizing if it was delivered by ravens (1 Kings 17:2–17)? Would it be safe to eat? Could you catch the "bird flu"? The thanks

are minimal. The opposition is significant, and the enemies are many. So far, so good? Or is this outside your wheelhouse?

As your training progresses, you will gradually find yourself so concerned about the needs of people that you will not care about anything else. Your own feelings will be replaced by concern for the needs of others. You will be on your way.

When Elisha had been called by God, he was plowing a field. He was not out lobbying to become the man of God. He had been handpicked by God, but he still had a choice. Did he want the job, or not? When he was found, Elijah "cast his cloak upon him." It was at that instant that Elisha knew he was being called by God, and it seems that he had no idea it was coming.

Whether or not he had ever entertained the idea of serving God, we do not know. What we do know is that he did not hesitate. Elisha delayed for only long enough to sacrifice his oxen. Elisha quickly accepted the calling and burned his bridges. The commitment he was making was permanent. There was no looking back. He would not see his parents again.

If Elisha's decision to follow God had a side effect on his immediate family or his friends, it was not a part of his decision. It was between him and God *only*. Whose oxen had Elisha sacrificed? Had they been his own or those of his parents? Whichever may have been the case, his parents had a half-plowed field and no oxen to finish the job. Side effects are not factored in.

God deals with people individually. Whatever other issues may be created by your choice that affect someone else will be dealt with in another way. They will not prevent God from moving his chosen person to the place of God's best for them.

Elisha had options. He did not have to accept the calling. He could have continued to plow, but he did not. He did not even finish the field he was plowing at the moment. The change was instantaneous. Elisha recognized it for what it was and moved on it immediately. Even at that early point in his relationship with God, Elisha understood that God would not wait while he delayed. It was then or never.

Many young people have taken their time about going into the ministry. We may need time for our walk with the Lord to grow, and an early choice might be difficult or impossible. However, when the time is right, the calling of the Lord may require a very quick response. The door of opportunity may be open for only a short time and you may have no way to know if that will be the case for you.

Milestones for the Student

Just because the door may be open for only a short time, that is not necessarily a problem. It may already be a part of your training. You are being trained to respond as soon as you understand that it has been the Lord whose voice you have heard. Hesitation is no longer an option. You are underway!

It would seem that at that early point, Elisha already had enough sensitivity to the movement of God that he understood the urgency of the choice at hand. The ability to hear the voice of God is crucial in ministering at a high level. If Elisha already had an extra measure of sensitivity to the voice of God, perhaps it had been a factor in his being called. Elisha would have had no control over that.

You have no control over what God may have already implanted into your spirit well before you came to know Him. In many ancient cultures, shamans were selected because of their high level of sensitivity to things taking place in the spiritual world. Perhaps this was the case in the calling of Elisha. We do not know.

What we do know is that God has created each of us with the ability to hear directly from Him. If you find that your ability to hear His voice is undeveloped or suppressed, that does not have to continue to be the case. You can begin learning to hear God, and the process will be the same as what your mentor has already undergone. You can do it!

While your calling may be equally important, it may not come in the way that it did for Elisha. In fact, the Lord will almost certainly have a never-to-be-repeated way to call you. It will be so special that you will have no doubt what has taken place. When that happens, the time to respond is upon you. You can accept or reject, but it will take place quickly and your life will be forever changed. Are you OK with that? God is.

As a newer Christian, I listened to the testimony of an older man who was describing the calling he had received in his youth. The church had a missionary serving in Africa as a speaker one day. My friend and mentor, Stan Wiberg, told of seeing a halo hovering above the missionary's head. It followed him wherever he moved on the platform. Stan was the only person to see it. He had never seen such a thing before and never saw one after that.

But at that moment, he knew that he was called to be a missionary to Africa. It was a unique calling; it was unexpected, and he had a brief moment to decide.

He turned it down. He stayed in Illinois and developed a successful lumber business. He married a Christian woman, had a family, and raised five children, all of whom were serving the Lord, and he became a generous supporter of missions. Long before I heard this, he had become an elder in the church. In other words, nothing bad had come from his refusal of the calling God had put on his life as a young man.

However, it was in *tears* that he told this story fifty years after it had happened. He fully understood that he had missed God's best for his life, and he was filled with sorrow. Stan had a single moment to accept or reject his calling, and he had felt bad about his decision for many years. The price for his choice was fifty years of regret.

Such a calling by God on a life is not extended to everyone. If you receive one, there may be only a short time for you to make your decision, and you may not know how long the door will be open. However, God will not open a door unless you are ready to make your choice. What is certain is that the door will not remain open indefinitely. Whatever you decide may be permanent. Do not take your calling lightly. You may be making an irreversible decision.

Consider the Consequences

You don't have to be fearful about this. Even though Stan had missed the Lord's best for him, he was never rejected by the Lord. God had blessed Stan throughout his entire life; he lived a full and productive life. God does not want to fill your life with stress. Relax. It will turn out OK.

Preparation to Minister Has Not Changed from Elisha's Day to This

God's method of training up his servants has not changed. The training is long and thorough and normally takes place as an understudy of a more experienced servant of God. Elijah was the mentor to Elisha, and Elisha became the mentor to his own young servant. Everyone had his day of preparation.

Today, that procedure may be more difficult. Where are the Elishas? Where are the mentors? I would submit that our churches have not done well at developing people with the discernment needed by a prophet. Do enough of our leaders function with fully developed discernment themselves? I suspect not. This is a sensitivity that has become somewhat lost to the church, and it needs to be recovered.

If our leaders lack sufficient discernment, they will be unable to mentor those who ought to be following. If you undertake to prime this sensitivity, you may find yourself without a mentor and have to go it alone. If you choose to travel this seldom traveled road, you may have to settle for learning directly from God. Would God be an acceptable substitute for a man? He is, and you will find that He is the ultimate mentor. With Him as your teacher, you may learn to minister in an incredible way.

Assuming you are successful at developing your discernment, you will probably discover that your new responsibility is twofold. You will use it to minister to the church. But you may also become responsible to mentor someone coming up behind you.

It is also somewhat common for a student to be unable to rise to a level higher than that of his teacher. In some situations, the first to establish a new ministry or even a business is not equaled by whoever follows. The entrepreneurial skills necessary to launch a new ministry are not identical to those needed to manage one that is already established. If we are to become increasingly effective as a church, those who follow must not be a watered-down version of ourselves. The person who follows should take it to the next level.

In business, an entrepreneur may very well launch a new business, while someone with managerial skills may follow to keep it going. God is not interested in maintaining the status quo. He is new every morning. He is always creating. What God has created is intended to be in an ongoing mode of expansion. How else is the world to be won? Expansion is to take place on two fronts. The lost are to be won and those already in God's camp are to continually grow. As a person of God, you will have a significant part in the development of both fronts.

One reason for a decline in effectiveness of the church is that each generation must have its own encounter with the Lord, and that does not always take place to the same degree that had been experienced by the previous generation. When there is such an encounter, it may not be of the same intensity that the last generation had experienced. In some cases, when God calls someone who has endured a very difficult past, his encounter with God can sometimes rise to a crisis level.

Perhaps the fact that God did not appear to intervene in his life at an earlier point may have provided an even better opportunity for him to understand just how unfortunate it is to live without God at the control wheel. If so, it would mean that God was already moving in his life, even while He seemed to be nowhere around.

It sometimes seems that for him, his crisis-filled background has prompted an extremely determined walk with God. He fully understands what it is like to be without God and is intent that nobody else should ever be forced to experience it. If the one who follows has not had such a difficult past, his ministration may not take the same form as that of his predecessor.

In God's world, training the next generation involves the trainee developing the same high level of determination to see God move as had his mentor. To mentor well, you will need to ensure that your student is not watching you alone but is watching and learning directly from the Lord. If you have had no mentor yourself, you will mentor without having experienced how such a relationship functions. However, if your student is also learning directly from the Lord, his effectiveness should not be diminished from your own level.

Releasing that person to enter his own ministry is a matter for discernment itself. While we know very well that God will continue to work in all of our lives, it is important to know when to release the student to launch his own ministry. When is he ready? The church is in desperate need of people with spiritual depth, and your understudy will be in demand.

Elisha continued as a servant for Elijah's entire ministry. The mantle passed to Elisha *only* as Elijah was being removed from the picture. Elisha had remained under the umbrella of his mentor until the very last second. Don't release your charge too early. He needs to go forward exceeding the level at which you have ministered yourself. Elisha received the double portion that he had asked of Elijah, and it only happened because Elisha clung tenaciously to his master until the very end.

Chapter 4

THE WAY TO RESTORE IT

Recognizing the Voice of the Lord

To recover discernment by reading about it in books may not be the best way to develop it. It is a feeling, a sensitivity not easily described, and it has to be experienced and exercised to allow it to grow. Even if it is felt, it still has to be recognized for what it is. God said, *"My sheep know my voice"* (John 10:27). The sheep know it, but the lambs may not. They might still need to learn to recognize it. One sign of a fully mature person of God is that he is able not only to hear but can have confidence in what step God wants him to take next. He knows what to do with the word he has received.

All of us have been created with a built-in sensitivity to God. It comes as standard equipment. It is not an extra cost option. However, that sensitivity can be seriously suppressed by the very loud and negative voices of worldly concerns. Nevertheless, it is not entirely lost. It can resurface with effort and training. That retraining becomes a major component in the growth process to Christian maturity.

While hearing the voice of the Lord is the first objective, it is only the beginning. The next step is to know what to do with the knowledge you have received. These two work hand in hand and are known as the word of knowledge and the word of wisdom. Few are able to operate in those gifts. Even in churches that believe these gifts are still available to them, many fail to go beyond the use of tongues and interpretation that are often the first experienced gifts.

Think about what you have seen take place in the word of God. Most cases about which a prophet is speaking will take place in the future. Can you think of a single case of a prophet speaking in tongues or interpreting? Tongues on the Day of Pentecost had a specific purpose, and they have a specific purpose today. However, they do not appear to be a tool used frequently by a prophet. He is moving in other gifts.

Even the use of the initially obtained gifts is sometimes not well understood and can result in an overemotional outburst not of God. One's prayer language can be mistaken for a message for the entire congregation. Most often, the church does not reject the message. Often those who are inclined to speak out with a word, ostensibly from God, already understand that what God speaks will be confirmed by His word.

Therefore, a message will usually pretty much reflect what God has already said in the Bible. The speaker may be only midway on his learning curve. If an emotional outburst is blurted out, it can actually be possible for someone to offer up a correct interpretation even though the message itself had not been a word given from God for that exact time.

Our elders, those who should sit in judgment over the service, must also further develop their own discernment. If the word spoken forth is from God, *is it also a word for this exact moment?* Judgment must confirm both issues. Many years spent in the word may enable an elder to recognize that a message does indeed line up with God's word, the Bible. That may be possible without a confirmation directly from the Lord. However, knowing if it is also a message for that exact moment can only be confirmed by a direct revelation from God. An elder is actually responsible for being able to confirm both on short notice. Those confirmations may come in two different ways and become a heavy responsibility.

Those who speak out, even incorrectly, have their hearts in the right place. But they may not have developed the sensitivity that Elisha had already received. When is this message needed? To move from operating in the initial to the later experienced gifts may not come about until proper use of the initial gift has been mastered. God will not speedily breeze someone through their time of training, and there are far fewer who are able to minister in the other gifts.

Our people may not find themselves becoming used in other gifts, and we need them to do so. For many, the necessary step can be as simple as slowing down and asking God if the message they are receiving is a message for today. Once use of the initial gift has been mastered, it will be time to move on to learn use of the next gift. You will be moved when you are ready.

Many today feel that spiritual gifts are no longer needed by the church. Hopefully, none of us will experience our city being surrounded by an army. However, being surrounded by the enemy may be either of a spiritual or a military nature. Even in Elisha's camp, the surrounding enemy was a physical army while God's own army was of a spiritual nature. God's army was ready to deal with either a physical or a spiritual enemy (2 Kings 6:17).

Those who doubt the availability of spiritual gifts would have no doubt that enemies still attack today at both the physical and the spiritual levels. Those same people would also have no doubt that God's army is ready and willing to enter the fight on our behalf at either level.

Even though we have God's promise that He will never leave us or forsake us (Hebrews 13:5), our old nature may still leave us with some doubt. *"I believe; help my unbelief"* (Mark 9:24). I think all of us have moments of doubt. It would be nice to know God's army was present also.

We understand that if we know, no faith is necessary. Obviously, if we are to *"live by faith and not by sight"* (2 Corinthians 5:7), we will have to move beyond where we are presently. However, God understands our weakness. A few instances of seeing clearly into the invisible realm of the spiritual world may make it easier to move to belief without sight. That was the case for the servant of Elisha. He was allowed to see God's army with his eyes. That was a special revelation that allowed him to see into the realm that he was not yet ready to perceive through discernment. Perhaps the next time, he would be ready to see without using his eyes.

If we are able to believe that God will fight on our behalf, should it be difficult for Him to communicate with us about it? God had wanted to communicate with the servant of Elisha enough that He provided a special means of doing so. He opened his eyes. If God would do something special for him, would He not also do something special for us?

Now that we have God's printed word, some may not make the connection with what God had done for the servant. It was not simply an event taken place in history. It was an actual event that greatly affected the life of a real person. That God had taken special measure to reveal Himself to the servant was a special act for him. The fact that we can read about it may not translate to our faith rising to the level necessary that we can believe and see during the course of our own lives. We may continue to need special revelations to help us grow our faith. We continue to need God's help just as much as Elisha's servant did, and it *is* available to us.

Elisha was able to exercise spiritual discernment. Without it, he would have had a problem on his hands. Without it, we may have a problem on our hands. The *need* for discernment has not been lost, and it remains available to those who are willing to develop it.

The Commitment

Training begins with commitment. That is evidenced by your willingness to leave your old life behind. You can't look back. Once you have gone through God's teardown, you will probably be unable to return to your former life. It will be gone forever.

Elisha had been plowing behind oxen in his family's field. The oxen were sacrificed and his parents were left behind forever (1 Kings 19:19–20). There was to be no vestige of his former life to fall back on. There was no turning back. It was a total commitment, and the willingness to have his former life go up in smoke (no pun intended—well, maybe a little one) is the evidence of his commitment.

The absolute commitment itself was one element that enabled the ministry of Elisha to rise to the level that it did. His commitment was total. For you to rise to a similar level, your commitment must also be total. You may be reluctant to completely abandon your former life, but you can readily see the effect it had on the ministry of Elisha, and it will be no different for you. Only when you are ready will God ask for your complete and total commitment. Once made, your commitment will open the door to great things.

You may recall that when Abram left his old country and traveled to the Palestine area, he had taken along his nephew Lot. However, the land promise was not given until Abram and Lot parted company (Genesis 13:8–10). To receive the promise of God, his old life had to be completely left behind. Lot had to go. It was not possible to hang onto even a small vestige of his former life. God is looking for total commitment.

Take a Break

If you are hesitant to make a complete commitment, Abram was no different. He took Lot along. God moved Abram slowly until he was ready to make such a commitment. When Abram finally gave up the

last little corner of his old life (his nephew Lot), the promise came. God will do that for you as well. If you give up your old life slowly, it's OK. God will move you along at the rate at which you are able to move.

It was only when Abram had left himself with no fallback position that his total commitment became evident. It was at that point that God began to move. The choice made by Elisha was only the first step. The intense training that followed his commitment would continue for many years.

Today, the initial aspect of training is the time invested in mastering the word of God. I don't believe that can be overstated. From the moment of your commitment, everything hinges on a well-developed understanding of God's word. Memorizing a large number of verses is not necessarily the objective. It is absolutely necessary to *understand* them, to have good recall, and lastly, to understand God. Understanding God, God's plan, and how He is likely to move in many different situations is what must be learned. To see the hand of God moving, it is critical to understand God, and that begins with an understanding of His word.

Many who are called have already been Christians for many years before there is a visible call placed upon their life. For them, they may have already begun to master the word of God. They have a head start. However the depth of understanding of God's word that is necessary to minister as a prophet will probably far exceed whatever level of understanding of the word they have already achieved. For even this group, many hours will be spent in the word while preparing to function as a prophet.

When I was a new Christian, a believer of great depth asked me what my favorite book of the Bible was. I quickly replied, "Genesis." I was at least in a position to have a favorite book at that early point in my own walk. He then asked if I had read the book of Genesis. I sort of felt that it was a stupid question. How could it have become my favorite book if I had not read it?

His next question caught me off guard. "How many times have you read Genesis?" I think I said, "Maybe three or four." He followed up with "You can't claim to have read a book until you have read it *thirty times.*" He was telling me that a casual reading would not provide the depth of understanding that is possible to acquire.

I decided to take his words as a challenge and began to read Genesis repeatedly. I don't think I ever reached thirty, but I began to see that there was far more in it than I had ever imagined, and I realized that every other book was no doubt filled with many tidbits I had never noticed. There is no way to short-circuit the learning process. It only comes with years of reading *and thinking* about what you have read. You'd better get started. I will not attempt to tell you that this can be done quickly. However, it is not just important; it is crucial.

The thinking part is easily overlooked. Many people can quote dozens of verses and may impress you with their knowledge. Can they also impress you with their understanding? If all they have seen is whatever the traditional interpretation of a verse has been, will they have seen all that there is to it?

There are many facets to God's word. You can read a passage many times, but suddenly an additional meaning will pop out at you. It was there all along, but it took repeated exposure before an unnoticed aspect of it came alive to you. The friend who said thirty readings was necessary clearly understood both the effort required and the potential for greatly increased understanding.

This is a matter for diligence.

> *Go to the ant, O sluggard, consider her ways, and be wise. Without having any chief, officer, or ruler, she prepares her bread in summer and gathers her food in harvest. How long will you lie there, O sluggard? When will you arise from your sleep?* (Proverbs 6:6 ESV)

A Thought for the Thinker

Get with it! Filling your very being with God's word is a matter for diligence. It cannot be done in a short time. Many hours, days, weeks, and years will have to be invested in careful study. The effort you will invest in learning the word may come at the cost of missing out on your former activities. Do you really want to go to all this trouble? If you do, I promise you will have no regrets. As you grow in the Lord, things that had been important will gradually fall away and will no longer be of interest to you.

The Day of Small Beginnings

Virtually everything provided as examples for us had its beginning in a very small way. This applies to more than one aspect of what God does in establishing a new ministry.

> *For whosoever has despised the day of small things shall rejoice, and shall see the plumb line in the hand of Zerubbabel.* (Zechariah 4:10 ESV)

First your ministry will have a very small beginning. You will minister to only one or possibly a small handful of people. You will hone your newly acquired skills on a small number of people, and it will gradually increase as you perfect your ministry skills and as you build a reputation as a reliable voice for God. This cannot be rushed. When you are ready, God will enlarge your ministry.

The Least of Men

The second way in which small beginnings will manifest themselves is that God selects the very least of those available as His servants. Gideon is an excellent example of this concept. He came from the smallest family in his tribe, he was the least among his own family, and he viewed himself as not up to his task.

> *"Please Lord, how can I save Israel? Behold, my clan is the weakest in Manasseh, and I am the least in my father's house." And the Lord said to him, "But I will be with you and you shall strike the Midianites as one man."* (Judges 6:15 ESV)

Manasseh was the younger son of Joseph and was the last to be born of all those who became the twelve tribes of Israel. Gideon had been born into what he viewed as the least of the twelve tribes. His clan was the weakest in his tribe and he was the least in his father's house. He was the least of men. Isn't that who God normally uses?

Was Gideon any different than we are today? He seems to have thought that to save Israel, God should have chosen someone else, someone with a more significant background, someone with military training, "anyone but me, please Lord." But the Lord had called him a "mighty man of valor" and had a totally different view of him than Gideon held of himself. The Lord was about to use him to accomplish His plan, and he was the very least of those available. God had chosen Gideon, knowing that he was the least of those available. Since God knew what He was doing, there must have been a reason for making that type of choice.

When Jesus was selecting His apostles, He *purposefully* chose men who were not esteemed as great. Some of them were fishermen—men of humble origin. He had chosen the least of men. It's when we know very well that we are unable to do on our own what God has called us to do that we are able to put it into God's hands and trust Him. Willingness to trust God is what makes the difference.

Even Jesus is portrayed as the least of men. He was born into a humble family in the smallest of towns. Not only was He born in the lowest of places in the entire community, a stable, but He was laid in a manger. What's a manger? It's a feeding trough. What lower place could He have been born into? He was not of noble birth. Even though He was the very son of God, He is still portrayed as being born in the humblest of circumstances. Once again, God knew what He was doing. Jesus could have been born under less humble beginnings, but Jesus had been born into the exact situation that the Lord regularly chooses: the least of men.

Sometimes those who have already demonstrated that they are unusually capable and have already accomplished great things will look to their own ability to help God along. That is the exact opposite attitude of what God is looking for. The very ability of those who are unusually capable may actually become a handicap for being used by God. For those blessed with natural ability, it may be even more difficult for them to look beyond themselves and turn to God.

Why does God deliberately choose the least of men? I believe it is to show that in the natural, what is about to happen is not possible. While God often chooses to work through a person, it is God who is ultimately bringing about His plan, not the chosen vessel. Man is unable to carry out the great work of God by himself, and that is most apparent when whoever God is using is obviously the least of men. God uses this method to make it possible for us to see that it was God and not man who is bringing about great things.

It's all about God. John the Baptist put it this way: "He must increase, but I must decrease" (John 3:30). John had it about right, but God was already big. We have to realize that He is already big and that we are small. It's only in our mind that God must increase.

Those who see very clearly that they are incapable of doing all that God requires are in a good position to be chosen. It is they who will pay very close attention to what God requires of them. They are the clay that can be molded by God; God is looking for the humble to be His servants. How do you feel about that? Are you inclined to brag about being humble? Better think about that one.

Bottoms Out

How low do you have to fall to be ready to be used by God? Are you willing to become the least of men? If you feel you are inadequate, you are right. That places you exactly where you need to be in order to be ready to be used by God. Being the least of men is not your excuse to sidestep God's plan for you. It is actually your qualification!

Are you able to set aside many years of preparation for some worldly position to become a servant of God? A minister acquaintance of mine had invested many years of preparation to become a petroleum engineer. He set it all aside to become a pastor. The joy that he experiences from his ministry far exceeds that which he had anticipated as a geologist.

How Nothing Is a Nothing

While God normally selects the least of men, there may be exceptions. However, everyone begins at ground zero. Those who may not have been the least of men, at first, are taken down a few notches, even as training is set to begin.

Have you considered the case of Moses, the greatest of the prophets? As we read about the great way in which God had used Moses, we see what appears to have been a very great man indeed.

Moses did not truly have the humble beginnings we might think God was looking for. Yes, he was the child of a humble Hebrew couple. However, he had been raised by royalty in the palace of the king of Egypt and I have heard it suggested that he was even under consideration as a possible pharaoh of Egypt. There's nothing humble about that. Yet for Moses to be used by God, he had to become the least of men.

There had to first be a complete teardown and rebuild. Moses had run for his life. He had left his royal beginning and become a herder of sheep in a foreign country. His eventual wife was a shepherd girl herself. Moses had very quickly been reduced from royalty to shepherd. He understood that he had become nothing, and he had forty years to think about it.

When he returned to Egypt, he was not well remembered by the Hebrews. He had killed an Egyptian and had fled for his life, leaving the Hebrews on their own—and they had forty years to forget him. There would have been a largely different generation alive when he returned. To the Hebrews, Moses was nothing.

Moses had no ability to resist the Egyptians; he had fled, had nothing remaining of his royal background, and had been gone for forty years. He had no power to stand against Pharaoh. To the Egyptians, Moses was also nothing. To all parties involved, Moses was nothing. The fall of Moses was extreme. He had gone from a prince of Egypt to a keeper of sheep in a foreign land. He had become the least of men.

In some cases, the magnitude of the fall somewhat reflects the level of the ministry that is to follow. Moses had experienced a larger than normal fall. That brought him to a good starting place. God was looking for the least of men, and Moses had become the perfect choice. His old life was behind. His new life found him living in a very humble state. Moses had become nothing. He may have thought that the rest of his life was to be spent tending sheep. He was probably unaware that he was under preparation to be used in such a significant way.

In becoming the least of men, Moses had *not* been stripped of his leadership ability at the natural level. God actually used that ability to organize and lead the Exodus. It was in his spirit that Moses had gradually been changed. To submit to God's voice and use his (God-given) natural ability, Moses had to learn both how to hear God's voice and how to restrain his old nature. He would use his natural ability only as it pertained to what God was doing for the Hebrews.

Since at the natural level Moses *was* highly capable, and since his abilities would be needed as the Exodus progressed, Moses was placed in an unusually difficult position. To be the least of men and still retain his leadership skills, Moses was being tested in a far more rigorous way than most. As difficult as it would have been, Moses was successful at both aspects of that unusual preparation. Perhaps that is partly why he is sometimes viewed as the greatest of prophets.

God treats us individually. What God had to do to prepare Mosses was tailored specifically to his situation. Your preparation will also be tailored specifically for you. If you have been called to become a servant of God, you are now aware that a humble background is called for. If you see your old life falling apart around you, will you view it as good news? It is.

God is preparing you for what lies ahead. It may not be easy, but it is necessary. You must be reduced to nothingness. Moses had lost his family, his friends, his position, his wealth, his possessions, and his future. Are you willing to have your former life fall completely apart around you? If you are, it will be worth it. Moses never looked back. He had found God's best and never questioned it. You can do the same. This is not to say that you should willy-nilly reject your former life. If that is necessary, God will show you how it is to be done.

Let's think about Joseph for a minute. Did Joseph even know there was a calling on his life. In his early years, Joseph is said to have had a coat of many colors. No elaboration of this is to be found in the scriptures. However, attention is given to its brightly colored appearance.

Likewise, the only gate into the tabernacle was brightly colored. The only gate symbolized the only way to God. The first gate (which led to the outer court) was available to everyone. Two additional doors inside the tabernacle signaled the ever-deeper progression into the heart of God. The farther in you went, the fewer people there were.

The prominently colored entrance is in stark contrast to the balance of the tent. However, it had a purpose. It was so that the only way to God would be easily seen. Jesus had referred to Himself as the door (John 10:9–16), the only way to reach God. God made the way in easy to spot.

Joseph would be mightily used by God in saving his family from starvation. He would be a savior of sorts. I am wondering if his coat of many colors may have been a metaphor for the brightly colored gate of the tabernacle, the only way to God. That brightly colored coat may have been pointing out that Joseph was to have been the only door to salvation for his starving family. Notice that his coat had been placed on him long before he had any idea of how he would eventually be used by God.

No matter how you feel about that, Joseph did have to endure much in order to be used in saving both his family and all of Egypt from starvation. The way of service to either God or to those on earth can be paved with pain and suffering. You might think this through before you file your application. Is it really worth it? Why should you care about others? Joseph had given up everything for them. Are you willing to do the same? I'll give you a hint. The reward is eternal.

Joseph was sold into slavery at seventeen years of age. He was a servant to Potiphar for five years and spent about five years in prison. He really had no choice in these matters and had done nothing wrong to boot. Would you regard all that time as training? For sure, it was a time of major testing.

As faithful as Joseph had been for his entire life, God still reduced him to nothing by using two pits. His brothers had deposited him in a well before selling him into slavery and Potiphar had put him in prison: two deep pits. While we are not told if Joseph experienced the same sort of doubt common to us all, we do know that he more than rose to the occasion. Did Joseph ever have the opportunity to accept or reject his calling? God's way led him out of prison and into a completely new life that allowed him to be used in a far greater way than what might have been the case for anyone else.

Do you think Joseph had any idea that he was being prepared for a really important job? We do not know the answer to that question. He had been a dreamer before being put in prison and continued to hear from God for his entire life. His sensitivity had an early beginning. Not just in his youth, but that sensitivity continued through his time of testing and ultimately became the vehicle that brought him out of prison and into the service of Pharaoh.

His dreaming was a factor in his brothers' hatred toward him and was the very thing that first caused him to land in two pits. That same dreaming was also the thing that catapulted him from prisoner to second in command over all of Egypt. At the same time, his dreaming had caused him to be hated by man and used by God.

The very thing that God sets out to use may be the very thing that is rejected by man. Man wanted to limit Joseph. God plans for him were without limit. How frequently does someone rise from prisoner to ruler in one jump? Only God could pull that off. Joseph responded, but God did it.

Perhaps there is a chance that the sensitivity possessed by both Joseph and Elisha prior to their obvious selection for use by God may have been a factor in their callings. People who have an extra degree of sensitivity to the spiritual realm are probably aware that they have it. If they are, it may be a clue for them that they may be singled out for special ministry in the future.

Joseph had already been able to hear God's voice while still a teen. Next, he had to learn to hear God's voice under the most difficult of circumstances: when he was in prison unjustly with God not moving to free him. How hard would that be? Is God out there? Why isn't He hearing me? Joseph continued to serve the Lord even when God seemed to be nowhere in sight. He was never distracted by unanswered questions. His commitment could not be shaken. He did not lose his focus. Wow!

Is It That Way Today?

Are you confident that God is with you at all times? Do you panic when you don't see his presence manifested around you? Trusting that He is there is a portion of the preparation needed to learn discernment. Believe first, then see. Not having Him noticeably present can actually be an opportunity.

The greatest of ministries may have to endure the greatest of tribulation as they are being prepared. A general rule might be the greater the calling, the more intense the preparation. Would you be up for that? If you can actually handle all of this, you may be on your way!

Joseph had been badly misunderstood. Observers may not understand prophets at all, so they probably will not understand that someone is going through preparation for something in the future either. You can expect to be misunderstood, both while you are in training and after you begin to function as a prophet. God, however, does understand. You will never have reason to doubt that. God understands.

You more than likely will undergo a lengthy time of preparation and have no control over how it proceeds. For Joseph, it was far from a fun-filled time. You should not expect to enjoy your preparation.

It would *not* seem that Paul had been the least of men. He had been highly schooled well before he was called. What happened to *him?* He was blinded. He was no longer able to see with his eyes and needed to see without them. Blindness was a special training device used exclusively for Paul. God had his immediate attention.

He had to unlearn what he already knew. His understanding at the natural level far exceeded that of most men. He could see very well with his eyes. Without them was a different matter. He had to see with his spirit. He learned this directly from Jesus even though Jesus was dead and gone. Jesus identified Himself to Paul *by name* (Acts 9:5). He did that for no one else in the entire Bible.

At that time, Paul had been an unbeliever (in Jesus as the Christ). However, upon being blinded, he immediately realized that it had been a *who* and not a *what* that had blinded him, and he asked who had done it to him. How frequently does someone actually have a conversation with Jesus before their conversion? He must have already had some level of discernment.

Once Jesus identified Himself to Paul *verbally*, he became a believer and worked with every bit as much energy to spread the gospel as he had expended to tear it down during his time of unbelief. It had been a radical conversion; blindness was the perfect confrontation for unbelieving Paul.

He was given specific instructions. Obedience was the initial requirement in his preparation. It was *only* after he followed his instructions that he was able to see with his eyes. The very first step in Paul's training required obedience, and it had begun even before his conversion. The Bible does not cover Paul's entire training. He spent three years in isolation.

Those years of solitude provided much time for thinking, praying, and seeing with his spirit. That time was necessary, even though he had already been a highly educated man. What God wanted to teach him was a far cry from what a university had to offer, and his training did not take place with his former associates looking on.

Does three years seem like a long time to go through training in isolation? How many years of previous training needed to be unlearned? How many years of schooling at the feet of God would follow? Are you up for a protracted time of training? How quickly would you be able to unlearn your previous learning? Paul did it, and you can too.

Am I making all this seem too difficult? How many of us are willing to follow God as carefully as his Old Testament prophets had done? God has not changed. People's needs have not changed, and the preparation of God's servants has not changed. What it took to become a man of God in the past is what it takes to become one today. The Old Testament prophets got through it and you can as well.

Take It slowly

Although this may seem to be difficult, your training will always be taken one day at a time. God will not overburden you with more than you can handle. He knows you better than you know yourself, and you will progress at a manageable rate. God will lead you through a training program specially designed for you and you alone. You can handle this!

The lives of most of us today are filled with activity and noise but little time for reflection. Even the gas pump wants to talk at me. Solitude and quiet times are needed to develop spiritual maturity, and they are in short supply. Growing spiritually may require purposefully seeking a quiet place.

While Paul knew more theology than any of the other apostles, he had to learn the application for much of it. What it says and how to apply it might be two different things. Once he could see the difference, he became the best teacher of God's word available to most of us. Much of our New Testament teaching comes from Paul. Without him, we would grasp far less from New Testament teachings. Paul was absolutely unique. Perhaps you may be too. You will never know until it happens.

Chapter 5

THE WAY IT CAN GROW

The Slow Spread of a Prophet's Influence

He put another parable before them, saying, "The kingdom of heaven is like a grain of mustard seed that a man took and sowed in his field. It is the smallest of all seeds, but when it has grown it is larger than all the garden plants and becomes a tree, so that the birds of the air come and make nests in its branches." (Matthew 13:31–32 ESV)

Those who bring up this verse are usually emphasizing the very small size of a grain of the mustard seed. They are surely correct to do this. It is another example of the day of small beginnings. As they continue to look into this parable, they are prone to leap to the end and see the very large, fully grown mustard tree. It is the huge change that has taken place that is often noticed. That also is a good observation.

However, what can easily be overlooked is the very long and slow growth process necessary for the tree to reach full maturity. The long time and small increments of the growth process are equally important components, as are the beginning and ending points. The story is being expressed as a metaphor alluding to the time needed to reach Christian maturity.

That time is probably more than you might anticipate. Are you good for the long haul? Things speedily learned might be speedily forgotten, while slower growth might stay with you better. God wants what you have learned to last for your entire lifetime.

While preparing my writings, I have gradually come to realize that even though my own background may have prepared me for some of what I have written, it has ultimately come to me from the Lord. I have managed to write some things that I would never have been able to come up with on my own. They have been given to me by God. They have been revelations.

Once I came to that realization, it also became clear that each revelation was small. I have never had a major revelation and have never been given an entire book or chapter at one time. God had been supplying me with thoughts in very small increments, never more than a paragraph and often only an individual word or sentence. Since they have been so small, it may have been somewhat easy to overlook that they have been important. If one is anticipating something big, it might be a disappointment to see nothing big happen all at once. Nevertheless, the small revelations together become large. God does provide something big; however, He may do it in small increments.

I have learned not to expect much at any one time. Once what I had been given was incorporated into what I was working on, something additional might appear. After I had gotten what was given right, more might be on the way. Most of the time, if I had two flashes come at once, I would not be able to remember the second by the time the first had had been roughed in. One is all I can handle. God knows me better than I know myself.

I believe the Lord supplies not just small beginnings but small additions all along the way as well. These small additions have a cumulative effect. God always has more for us, but it probably will not be dropped into our lap all at once. More comes when we are ready for it.

Use what you have been given, and more will come. God has an unlimited supply and is generous with it. However, he wants to know you will be a good steward and will not unload on you all at once. What appears to an outsider to have been a major revelation may have actually been a series of small tidbits of information that at first may not even have seemed to be connected at all.

When you realize that you have had a revelation from God, it may not mean that you are finished. Continue to stay tuned. There may be a lot more that is still to come. The number of very small additions can be many, and the cumulative effect makes the final result become large.

In my own case, quite a bit of what God gives me comes during the night. It is at those times that my mind is uncluttered with many other issues. When my mind is clear, it is more possible to hear from God. At those times, I am not even struggling to hear from God; it just comes. When it does, I have to either get it written down immediately or wake up enough to think about it for a while so that I can remember it in the morning. If I don't, it may be gone forever. What God supplies generously must be used, or it may become lost.

For the past several years, I have found myself in need of hearing aids. For the most part, I can hear reasonably well when only one sound is present. When multiple sounds are coming at me all at once, I have trouble. It can be difficult to sort out those sounds and tune in to the most important. A lot gets missed. I need quiet time to hear, both physically and spiritually. One voice at a time is all I can handle.

To hear from God, one must clear one's mind of everything else. Even if God is speaking all along the way, it is only when the mind is uncluttered that God can be heard. God speaks with a single voice, and one must learn to hear Him when many other voices are also speaking at the same time.

King David, though not a prophet, still had to undergo a gradual increase in his sphere of influence. He was not elevated to king until his leadership had been developed, tested, and proven. Only when his people understood that he was ready to lead did he become king. This took time.

I believe the leadership principles learned by David also apply to many different situations. David had served under Saul for many years. When he was ready to lead, he broke with Saul and stepped out alone. He had no supporters. It began with David hiding in a cave from Saul, who was determined to track him down and kill him. It had not been an easy road to leadership.

We regard his first command as having been launched at the cave Adulum (1 Samuel 22:2), where those who first came to him were "everyone who was sick or in debt." Four hundred came at first, and they were not trained solders; they were the least of those available (where have you heard that before?) and did not come to help David. They needed help themselves. While it was a pretty ragtag bunch, it was a beginning. David accepted them and his following grew. The route to having your own needs met may very well be to help the other guy first. *"Give and it shall be given to you"* (Luke 6:38).

At Ziklag, David found himself with six hundred followers (1 Samuel 30). Eventually many more became his supporters and many of those were well-trained military people;

they were the sort of an army David would have needed. Toward the end, support grew to a flood and David was eventually elevated to king. It began slowly but picked up momentum as it progressed.

If you remember how David's story developed, even Adulum was not the beginning. David had to first learn to fight while tending sheep. He had fought and killed the lion and the bear (1 Samuel 17:34–36). Next, he single-handedly took on Goliath, the biggest and fiercest the Philistines had, and killed him while making it look easy (1 Samuel 17). His preparation had begun even before he understood his eventual calling.

God had begun to prepare him long before David knew there would ever be a significant call on his life. He honed his leadership skills while serving under Saul, and by the time David ran from him, he was well prepared to lead. Even David had been reduced to nothing, and it was done while he was not even attempting to become something. To be elevated to leadership on his own, a significant change was needed. Even after having received so much special preparation, he still had to begin in a small way. He was hiding in a cave.

If you continue down the road to become a prophet, you will probably find yourself making a clean break with your past and you will establish your ministry from scratch. Since few are available, you may not be trained under another prophet. Some of what you proclaim will also represent a break from how those in your former place operated. Perhaps you will be called upon to minister to the very ones who have opposed your ministry as a prophet.

If They Did It, You Can Do It

You may have an uphill fight on your hands. At first, you may have little recognition. Are you ready to throw in the towel? You don't have to give up. Joseph survived it. Moses survived it. David survived it. Paul survived it. Elijah survived it, and so did Elisha. You can too.

A Review of the Principles Needed to Function as a Prophet

- Training begins with a well-developed *understanding of God's word.*
- God selects the very *least* of those available as His servants.

- Each revelation is *small.*
- The calling of the Lord may require a very *quick response.*
- *Use* what you have been given, and more will come.
- Long and *slow growth* is necessary to reach full maturity.
- You can expect to be *misunderstood.*
- It is only when the *mind is uncluttered* that God can be heard.
- You may be asked to *mentor* the next guy.
- You will need to learn *when to listen, how to hear, and how to respond.*
- You must perceive *what form of communication* God is using.
- The route to receiving from God may very well be to *give first, then receive.*

Listening, Hearing, and Speaking

As a young Christian, I was fortunate to have attended a live meeting and healing service of healing evangelist Katherine Kuhlman. I have also watched many of her television broadcasts. Those programs are no longer aired and few of us old geezers who had seen her are still around. If I remember right, she passed away in 1976.

Younger people coming up have not had the opportunity to observe her ministration. At a Christian Booksellers Convention many years after her passing, one vendor was playing a video of one of her meetings. Two younger people watched intently for a few minutes and left while saying, "I had always wondered what she was like." They were in a hurry and left having only seen the way she appeared to them physically. They had passed by an opportunity to learn from her even long after her death.

There are those who thought that Katherine Kuhlman was a little strange. The same has been said about Aimee Semple McPherson, whose ministry had preceded that of Kuhlman. That's OK. Elijah would surely be looked on as strange if he were around today. Such people of God do not attempt to conform to the social norms of their day. If they seem to be outcasts from their own, it makes sense. They were so focused on God that they gave little consideration to the world in which they lived. They were truly "in the world, but not of the world."

However, Kuhlman was not strange; she was intent. She would always concentrate on hearing the voice of God and tried very hard to stay in tune with what God was doing in her service. It was not that she was hoping that God would move; she was *absolutely certain* that God was on hand and about to move.

Will You Seem Different?

Would you be OK with your ministry causing you to seem like a weirdo to those around you? Those greatly used by God had no problem with that. If your focus is entirely on God and nothing else, you will care less how you appear to others. You won't even give it a second thought.

She had no hesitation that God would use her, and she wanted to be sure not to miss Him. She listened intently so as not to miss anything and knew that He was there. She knew that He was just about to do something special and had to be careful not to take off on her own and miss what God was about to do. She may not have a second chance.

While working as a radio announcer during college, I was taught that we should have no "dead air." Every second was to be filled with sound. People would begin leaving the station within seconds if silence prevailed, and the station could not risk losing its audience. It would be very slow in rebuilding. For radio, dead air was a bad thing.

I am thinking that the church has somewhat the same attitude. When the singing stops, announcements are quickly made. When the preacher says amen, the choir hits the downbeat of the next song. As the last note falls quiet, someone blurts out with a message. There is no dead air, no quiet time, no waiting on God.

I believe that for the church, there are times when dead air is a *good* thing. Dead air means no talking and perhaps we are talking when we should be listening. The church might be as good a place to hear from God as any. Isn't that why we came? We should come expecting to hear from God.

When we hear from our pastor, we are most likely hearing from God. His job is to present us with God's teaching for us that day. More than likely, our pastor has made a significant investment of time in preparing a word for us. That's a good thing. But should we be solely dependent on what he may have for us? What would be wrong with hearing directly from God. He is up for it. Are we?

As I occasionally overhear conversations involving several people, it is common for everyone to be speaking at once and no one is listening. Nobody is being heard. If we are talking, we are not listening. If we are not listening, we are not hearing. If we are not hearing, we will not know what God may want to do. Missing God is a bad thing. "God, You'd better move quickly because good, bad, or otherwise, we're moving on. We've gotta beat the crowd to the restaurant."

What's wrong with a little dead air? If nothing is truly taking place, perhaps dead air is undesirable. But what if something *is* happening? Not all communication is audible. Most of us can read facial expressions or body language to some extent. Those are silent. Even at that, with no written word, no facial expression, no body language, and no spoken word, it is still possible to communicate directly with God. That will take place spirit to spirit, and that is very quiet indeed.

Katherine Kuhlman had no fear of a little dead air. For her, hearing the voice of God was the most important thing in the entire service. *Nothing* was going to take place unless it was from God. She *would not* move until she had heard from God. For her, dead air was no problem. I have seen her stand silently while listening intently and waiting for perhaps as much as thirty seconds at a time. What the congregation thought about that was of no concern.

When she heard from God, the people would hear from her. She was God's voice in the sanctuary. When she spoke, people would know that God had spoken. There was no doubt about it. I cannot remember seeing any minister of God or layperson who experienced a more regular or mightier working of God. She knew when to listen, how to hear, and how to respond.

The results speak for themselves. Kuhlman was widely regarded as having had a major healing ministry. She did. Many were healed. Droves had come to her meeting while hoping to see someone healed, and they were never disappointed.

However, the most important aspect of her ministry may have been misunderstood. What is often overlooked is the huge number of people who came forward at the altar call. In interviews, the idea that there had even *been* an altar call might not even be mentioned. Nevertheless, the visible, the spectacular, the healing was important; but it was secondary.

When a paralytic was brought to Jesus, He said, "Your sins are forgiven." Since the man had been brought forward seeking healing, most were shocked at Jesus's words. He knew exactly what everyone was thinking and responded to their silence.

For which is easier to say, "Your sins are forgiven," or to say, "Rise and walk"? But that you may know that the son of Man has authority on earth to forgive sins"—he then said to the paralytic—Rise, pick up your bed and go home. And he rose and went home. When the crowds saw it, they were afraid and they glorified God, who had given such authority to men. (Matthew 9:5–6 ESV)

Jesus had used the more spectacular and more visible to call attention to everyone's greater need: salvation. What nobody had been thinking about, Jesus pushed to the forefront, and the spectacular had prepared everyone to hear the less spectacular, but more importantly, that their sins could be forgiven.

Katherine Kuhlman was using a tactic similar to that of Jesus. While she did not go so far as to publicly forgive someone's sin, as Jesus had done, she did use healing to get their attention. People had come hoping to see a miracle, and they did. When they witnessed a miracle, the crowd was seeing the power of God in action. The results of a healing were immediately visible. However, the results of a person's sin being forgiven would only become visible as the person's life began to exhibit the slow change that would gradually follow.

The healing ministry was the way that God revealed Himself. When people saw the power of God, they saw God. Then realizing that God was both real and had real power, they were then able to believe God for their own salvation. At Kuhlman's meetings there were many *hundreds* more responding to the altar call than had been healed. I believe she had been more widely used by God in winning the lost than in bringing healing. It's fine to remember the spectacular, the healing, but perhaps we don't remember how many were saved in her meetings. The greater purpose for the healing meetings had been to win the lost.

Why Am I Here?

Your job as a prophet will be to know God's ultimate purpose for His people. The immediate need is probably important. However, God's greater plan has always been and always will be to reach the entire world. You dare not lose sight of His greater purpose. You will be right in the middle of it.

The Difference between Listening and Hearing

People sometimes think they are unable to hear the voice of God. That may not be the case at all. The time to hear is when God is speaking. If you are doing the talking, you may not be doing the listening. What needs to be learned is when to be silent. "When is that?" you ask. When you feel that God is about to move, it might be time to stop, be quiet, wait on God, and listen. You might just hear better when you are listening. You will need to learn when to listen, how to hear, and how to respond.

A prophet is expected to recognize the voice of the Lord regardless of what form it takes. This goes beyond listening. It's about hearing, which is not quite the same thing.

> *And he said, "Go and stand on the mount before the Lord." And behold, the Lord passed by and a great and strong wind tore the mountains and broke in pieces the rocks before the Lord, but the Lord was not in the wind. And after the wind an earthquake, but the Lord was not in the earthquake. And after the earthquake a fire but the Lord was not in the fire. And after the fire the sound of a low whisper. And when Elijah heard it, he wrapped his face in his cloak and went out and stood at the entrance of the cave. And behold there came a voice to him.* (1 Kings 19:11–13 ESV)

How foolish would it be to "stand before the mount" with a wind strong enough to break the mountain apart? Such a wind would blow you right off the mountain. Would you run for your life if an earthquake started around you? Are you up for being in the midst of a fire? Those incidents are being expressed using hyperbole. The wind was not strong enough to break apart a mountain. A man would be unable to stand in the face of such a wind. However violent, it was not strong enough to break the rocks apart.

We are not being told how violent the wind was but how intently the prophet was listening for the voice of God. He listened past the distractions to hear the voice of God. The wind, the earthquake, and the fire were very loud voices, but Elijah did not mistakenly think any of them were the voice of the Lord. The prophet would not allow the violent or spectacular to cause him to lose focus and fail to hear the quieter voice of the Lord.

When the sound of the low whisper came, he instantly knew that he was hearing the voice of the Lord and he responded immediately. Some versions word this phrase "the still small voice," causing many to think that the Lord will speak very quietly. He may very well do just that. However, it is not the decibel level of His voice that is critical.

During a recent church service, I had felt a momentary nudge that I should go to the altar. It was not audible at all and lasted for only a matter of couple of seconds, and then it was gone. It had been God attempting to move me. I had hesitated, failed to respond, stayed in my place, and missed God. I have no idea what God would have had for me that day. The voice that day had been a very brief nudge, a feeling, and nothing more. The problem for me was that I had hesitated *after* I realized that it was God

God has said that He would make us fishers of men. Might He be looked on as a fisher of men Himself? If so, what type of fisherman might He be? He would not be a bait fisherman who dangles a worm in front of a fish for long periods hoping that the fish would eventually decide to bite. Perhaps He is more like a fly fisherman who very lightly and carefully casts his fly on the water and leaves it for only a brief moment before moving it to another spot. God will light for a very brief moment. When God calls, a quick response is necessary. God is moving on.

If we are to hear from God, we have to learn to respond not only to "the still small voice" but also to one that is very short-lived. God may wait for us as we attempt to hear Him. But once we recognize His voice, we are expected to respond immediately. Until I learn to respond as soon as I hear His voice, He will not move me to the next level.

I believe that when we are not being heard, we talk louder if not shout. We want to ensure that we are being heard. It usually works. When we speak loudly, people pay attention. God does not operate that way. When God speaks, we will not be required to listen. We have to be willing. Only if we listen will we hear His voice. God knows very well that if we do not care enough to listen, neither will we care enough to respond. Why should He bother to speak when He knows full well that He will not be heard? Believe it or not, He is probably still speaking.

Even though God may not speak more and more loudly, He does not give up easily. If we are reluctant to hear God, He may bring us to the same point repeatedly. The circumstances may change, but the same lesson will repeatedly confront us. God may continue to teach us whatever principle we are in the midst of learning until we get it right. He will not move us to the next lesson until we have learned the one we are on.

Do you feel like you're stuck in the same old mold? Maybe you'd better listen up. You may have been missing God all along. The good news is that God has more patience with us than we may have with Him.

It is the *nature* of His voice that must be recognized, and it may not have the same volume at each encounter. A seasoned prophet will not be concerned whether God's voice is loud or quiet. That is subject to change. However, the nature of God is unchanging, and it is how His nature is reflected in His voice that must be spotted. Just because we understand that God is the same yesterday, today, and forever (Hebrews 13:8), it does not also mean that He will speak in the same way each time we hear from Him.

Many of us anticipate that God will always show up in the same way that He has in the past. Our culture pushes us in that direction. We see weekly television programs that are run on the same day and hour. Those of us who are students attend classes on a regular schedule. Our bills come due at the same time each month. Our expectations have become habitual. All that tends to leave us expecting to hear God in the same way and at the same time as He has spoken previously.

That may be the way the world works. God, however, has His own way and His own time. He does not necessarily work according to a schedule. He will appear at exactly the right moment, but don't expect it to be on a timetable that you might anticipate. If we are looking for God, thinking that He will appear in the same way or time that He did yesterday, we will often miss God. He specifically avoids permitting an undiscerning follower to permit yesterday's meat to become food for today. Yesterday's meat might well have rotted by the time tomorrow comes. Yesterday's meat was for yesterday; today's meat is for today. God has fresh meat for us daily.

The mana collected by the Hebrews during the Exodus was only good for one day. This is an allegory showing the need for the fresh touch from God for today. We need a new touch from God each and every day. We need new mana daily (Exodus 16:35), and God will always have a special word for us for today.

The Hebrews had to gather mana each day. They had to expend an effort to gather it. Even though God supplied, the people still had to do their part. It was there. It was free, and there was no limit as to how much they were allowed to collect each day. But if they didn't gather it, they would have none at all.

God supplies everything. That's His part. It's free, and we can collect as much as we wish. However, the collection necessary is our part. If we fail to expend the effort to collect it, it will go ungathered. When God speaks, rarely is it truly unilateral. We always have a part. Even though our part is very small, at a minimum, we will have to receive it. As small as that may seem to be, our failure to do it is often the very thing that causes us to not hear from God.

Don't Force It!

Today, that minimal part translates to us expending the effort to listen for the voice of God. We need to have our spiritual antennas up to receive God's word for today. That's our part. He speaks. We listen. Isn't this easy?

Is God the same yesterday, today, and forever (Hebrews 13:8)? He is. Does He show up at the most critical moments? He does. Can we have confidence that He will be there for us? Absolutely. Does that mean He will have the same word for us today that He did yesterday? Possibly not.

None of us would want to miss God. Exodus 33:22 says, *"God passed by."* He didn't linger indefinitely. He was there, but it was momentary. While he is always available, there are times when He is especially within reach. It is at those brief times that we need to be ready. If we are unable to sense when God shows up, He will be long gone before we even attempt to find out what He has for us today.

When He does show up, something may be about to happen. He will either be listening to you or He may have come with instructions. Either way, you are about to hear from God. God is ready to move. Not listening for Him will result is missing Him as He passes. Repeatedly missing God will eventually lead to many unanswered prayer requests. Many unanswered prayers will eventually cause one to stop praying. If it doesn't work, why bother? It will create doubts that God will or even can move on your behalf. Doubts that continue to fester may eventually lead to unbelief.

When God shows up, that is also the time to lay your petitions at His feet. However, the sequence is critical. Listen first to what He may be saying to you. If God has showed up for the purpose of bringing a word to you, hear it. Only after God has spoken should you bring up your own requests. Being willing to set aside your own concerns and listen shows that hearing from God is more important to you than making your requests.

What He wants to say is more important than what you might want to say yourself. Be assured God already understands your needs and wants to supply them. You may not need to blurt them out. Once you have heard from Him, you may find that you no longer have needs. Let God speak first, then it's your turn.

Conversely, frequent answered prayer will prompt one to pray more readily and believe for results. Hearing from God regularly will result in spiritual growth and an understanding of how God works. We need the word of God for *today!*

It is possible to think you are listening when in reality you are not. Even among established prophets, there is still the possibility of losing focus and making a bad call. When Israel pleaded to Samuel for a king, Samuel anointed Saul, who was head and shoulders taller than anyone else. The Hebrews had made the mistake many of us make. They accepted Saul based on his stature. They were looking in the wrong place. God looks on the heart, not on physical appearance, and the Hebrews expectations were centered on the external. He had not been God's choice. However, God had given them the kind of leader they wanted, a worldly leader, and their poor choice caused the entire nation of Israel to suffer.

Will You Hear from Your Boss?

When you become God's prophet, you will stand before your boss and be accountable for your ability to hear from Him. Can you do it? God knows that you can. He would not have chosen you if you could not. The question is not "Can you hear from God?" You can! However, will you hear from Him? That is the question.

The Word

There are two aspects to our spiritual growth through which you can progress *partially* due to your own effort. The first is our understanding of God's word, the Bible. You can dedicate yourself to its reading, and over time, you can absorb a great deal. There! You do not have to relinquish complete control. However, even in that area, you can't really go it alone. You read; God reveals. With God, everything is a two-way street.

If you have not been strong in the word, you can fix that. The key to your success is incremental growth. Any attempt to take a gargantuan leap from being weak to becoming strong all at once will probably result in failure. If you have been amazed at an occasional saint who regularly spends four hours in the word, an attempt to replicate his habit will most likely backfire.

Your first step should be to form a new habit of daily time in the Bible. Your first goal is not to increase your time. Consistency is the issue. Some find it helpful to have a specific time and place to do their reading. Having a quiet place in your home can be an effective tool for use in solidifying your new habit. Having a regular time and place will ease the difficulty of forming a new habit of daily reading.

Forming a new habit of daily reading will take thirty days. Once you have formed the habit of daily reading, you can then gradually increase the time dedicated. However, don't allow it to become drudgery. It's better to read five minutes and learn from it than to read for thirty and struggle. If you enjoy it, you'll remember the word; if it's drudgery, you'll remember the struggle.

If it becomes difficult, you will give up and not read at all. While I advocate reading far more than five minutes, first develop a habit of consistency, and then worry about the time. After thirty days of reading for five minutes, consider increasing your time.

You might expect some opposition to this. There is always opposition to any ministry, but it is especially common among new ministries. Don't become dismayed by this. It's actually a good thing. If you find opposition to your effort to grow in God, it means you are doing something right. You can actually rejoice when you encounter it.

When you reach fifteen minutes, new doors will gradually open. Your well-established habit can gradually be broadened, and as you do, you might eventually divide your time into four types of readings. First, I would suggest reading the Bible straight through. Reading that way for fifteen minutes daily should allow you to complete the Bible *easily* in a single year. Multiple times through will likely prompt you to read several versions in their entirety.

Second, I support the concept of initially becoming extremely well versed in one book. The person who encouraged me to read the book of Genesis thirty times had a good plan.

The more you have read a specific book, the more will pop out at you and you will become amazed at how much there is to be discovered. You will realize that the entire Bible is filled with never-before-noticed truths, and you will leap with joy as you find them.

Third, whenever you have occasion to turn to a specific verse, don't just read *it*. Read a larger portion, including verses both before and after the verse you have looked up. Learning the context and additional meaning will make the entire passage clearer.

Fourth, your time of reading can also become a devotional time. Forming a new habit of devotions will go hand in hand with learning to understand God. Some advocate spending large amounts of time in scripture memorization. I am fine with this, but I don't regard it as essential (as a large-scale effort). If you actually read a portion thirty times, you will come close to having memorized it. I like to place the emphasis on gaining an understanding.

I have suggested that you divide your time in four ways.

1. Read the Bible completely through.
2. Become an expert on one book.
3. Do a thorough study on each passage you open.
4. Use a portion of your time reading to have devotions, a time of communion with God. In these quiet times, you may gradually find that while you are speaking to God, you may discover that you are having confirmations from Him.

By the time you have expanded into these four ways of reading, you may find that your time has gradually increased until you are spending forty-five minutes daily in your reading. If you have increased without really noticing it, you have succeeded in forming and expanding a much-needed habit.

Even forty-five minutes is a far cry from the four hours spent by some who would still be far advanced from where you would be. However, forty-five minutes is far more than many Christians invest and you will be growing quickly at that point. Good for you!

Did I say to divide your time four ways? There is also a fifth way. Reading is only half of the battle. Thinking is the other half, and it is probably equally important as the reading itself. Don't just read. *Think.*

If you want to appear to be very spiritually oriented, while you progress, perhaps you might use the word *meditate* instead of *think*. Thinking is for average folk. Meditation is for philosophers. Either way, you've got to digest what you read. Look past the language used by people who lived thousands of years ago and ask yourself how this would be said if it was being written today. What is the meaning of what you are reading? Ask God to show you new things that you have never noticed, and He will do it.

If you speed-read through it, you *will* learn. However, you will profit far more by reading for ten minutes and then spending another ten thinking (or meditating, if you must) about what you have read than you will by reading for twenty minutes without stopping. You will probably quadruple your learning if you spend as much time thinking as reading.

Some will attempt to tell you that the Bible says what it means and means what it says. In other words, every word is to be taken at face value and no allowance is necessary for cultural or nonliteral-language devices. I think we would all admire that level of dedication.

However, if you have difficulty understanding a passage, it may be due to the way the ancient writers thought and used words. They were not always used in the identical way that we might use them today. Understand the Bible is true (accurate) and can be understood even when it requires extra effort.

This Ain't No Big Deal!

No matter what your place is, you will need to develop a good grasp of God's word. That is expected of all of us. You don't need to do this because of a possible calling to the ministry of the prophet. It will be needed no matter where you end up.

Prayer

The second area in which you can affect control over your walk with God is prayer. As was the case with time spent in the word, an incremental increase will be the road to building a stronger prayer life. For many, prayer may have been limited to specific moments when we know that prayer is expected. Table grace and prayer during worship services or communion are common ones. While those times are important, they are not at the heart of our prayer life at all. My own testimony may offer suggestions as to how to build a time of prayer as well as what might be included.

I remember, as a new Christian, my wife and I attended a Saturday night prayer meeting. For us, even being involved in something like that on a Saturday night was a significant change. How do you spend your Saturday evening? Would it be sacrificial to attend a prayer meeting? Would you even consider being involved in one? Couldn't some other time of the week be just as good for prayer? Have fun on Saturday night and pray when nothing better is going on? Is that OK, or does it bring conviction? Where does prayer fit in your priorities? Time is something of a commodity. If you offer your best to God, you just might receive His best in return.

What I did not initially understand was the degree to which the Saturday night prayer meeting had a direct impact on the Sunday morning service. After attending several times, I was able to see a direct correlation between the intensity of that prayer meeting and what took place on Sunday. That it took place the night before was a definite factor. I believe the Lord had honored the sacrifice of our Saturday nights. The Saturday night prayer meeting is the most important meeting of the entire week and sets the stage for Sunday worship.

There may be many times that we wonder if God really does answer prayer. The good news is that we sometimes receive such an unmistakable answer that all doubt about that evaporates. The way in which prayer offered on those Saturday nights was answered has caused my confidence in prayer to last for these many years.

We often remember specific ways that God has answered. This was different. We never knew what God had in store for us the next morning, but a pattern emerged. A high level of intensity during that meeting aways seemed to result in something special taking place on Sunday. It was with great joy that we arrived on Sunday knowing that we would see God at work.

The meeting was not led or even attended by the pastor. Had he attended, he would have been expected to play a major role and would have had a big influence on it. I eventually learned that the pastor had enough confidence in his prayer warriors to avoid this meeting. The meeting was led by its participants. Average people had a direct and significant part in what took place during the Sunday service.

Perhaps your prayer today is similar to what I experienced as a new Christian. I didn't have much of a prayer. A new Christian may not have given a great deal of thought to what he might pray about, and as a result, he runs out of ideas very quickly. Many people who are just beginning to establish a prayer life can pray for only about fifteen seconds.

As I watched mature Christians pray on and on and really only stop to allow someone else a chance to raise his voice, I was amazed that someone might have been able to pray for the entire evening without even stopping to take a breath. I gradually learned they had not reached that point overnight. I was in the presence of long-standing prayer warriors.

Knowing that I would only have a very short prayer, at first I was reluctant to pray out and have the rest of the group realize that I had only a fifteen-second prayer. I was trying to compare myself to more mature believers. As my courage grew, I gradually became willing to pray out and was surprised to see that the entire group welcomed my prayer. I was never looked down on because I was just learning to pray. They understood where I was and were excited to watch me slowly improve my own prayer life. They were very encouraging, and nobody was concerned that my prayer was short. Everyone had liberty to pray his own prayer, and everyone did just that.

There was no plan of attack. Everyone prayed out loud in no special order. Nobody seemed to decide who would pray first or when the meeting would end. However, one man stood out from the rest. Solomon Johnson was perhaps the oldest person in the group. He was nearly always the one to first break out into prayer, and pray he did. On bended knee, he prayed with every fiber of his being while crying out to God. The joy he felt as he prayed was evident to everyone. That man knew how to touch God. It took me some time to realize just what a privilege it had been to sit in his presence while he prayed.

The interesting thing was that everyone seemed to know when the meeting was over. Even I could sense it. The burden would lift and the entire atmosphere would lighten up. It was time for cookies.

I learned quite a lot by attending those meetings. I took my first steps in learning how to pray. I began to sense the presence of God, and I had the beginnings of knowing when a change was taking place. There was never a time when anybody stepped up and said, "Mike, this is how you do it." It was my involvement that became my teacher. That will be the way for you as well. Get involved in the things of the Lord.

If you feel that you will be uncomfortable in an unfamiliar situation, at first you might, but so what? It didn't take me long to feel like I belonged, and as I gradually became involved, God began to open my eyes and I was able to begin learning. Being hesitant to step into unchartered territory is normal. However, it doesn't have to rule your life. God will honor your willingness to step up wanting to learn more about Him. If you make yourself available, God will use you, even when you are new.

Are you able to sense the presence of God? All that was new to me, but I soon became able to feel the burden of prayer and could tell when it lifted. At that early point in my life, I was beginning to sense the presence of God. It was also the beginning of hearing from Him. Those small advances might have seemed minor. Not so. They were foundational.

I have brought up the idea that beginnings are small and that incremental increases are also small. As we exercise our limited ability, things expand. My own prayer got gradually longer, and my ability to sense the presence of God increased. Not only that, but in some measure, I experienced the beginnings of sensing when God was *about* to move. The confirmation often came the following morning.

You may be in a position of not really knowing where to begin or how to proceed. That's OK. As a new believer, how could you? If you begin in the middle, you will have at least begun. The important thing is to begin. If you run out of something to pray about, it's OK. You're done. However, as you become more comfortable, you will think of more and more to include in your prayer.

God will be listening to the cry of your heart, not to the technical excellence of your prayer. If you are on the high side of your learning curve, you may begin by bringing up your personal prayer requests. If you do, they will be heard. Will you be ready to believe that God will respond? In due course, that will come. At first, you may have some doubt, even as you pray. All of us sometimes experience doubt. Just don't let it stop you. As you forge ahead, you will find your belief growing.

As you pray, you will also build your own faith. As you build your faith, you will begin to hear from God. As you begin to hear from God, your faith will grow even more. It will be something akin to a spiral effect. However, it all depends on your willingness to begin even though you are uncertain how or where to start.

Prayer does not need to be 100 percent requests. When you are speaking to God, you don't always have to be asking for something. If you begin by offering praise to God, the upshot is a little different. If you tell God that He is good, that He is loving, that He is all knowing, that He is the creator, that He is the healer, and that He is the author and finisher of your salvation, you are putting God in perspective. You will begin to realize just how capable God actually is, and it will become much easier to expect Him to answer your prayer. You think the praise is for God? It is. However, it also helps you.

As you put Him in perspective, He becomes larger and larger. You are recognizing what He can do. The larger He becomes, the more easily you can move to belief. What He has done, He will do. As He grows in your eyes, your faith grows, your problems become smaller and smaller, and it becomes far easier to expect your prayer to be answered. Your unbelief vanishes, and your faith increases. As your faith increases, there is no longer room for doubt. That's when God begins to work.

You may find yourself working from a mental list of several areas you want to cover, such as your Sunday service, the health of your friends and relatives, jobs for those who are out of work, youth ministry, missions, the state of our political climate, and many others. Each of those areas may bring to your mind a few specific needs. Even if you pray for three seconds for each of the needs you think of, the number may surprise you. Your fifteen-second prayer may have just been catapulted into several minutes.

If you are praying in a group, you may begin by taking up prayer requests. When praying out loud, the first person who prays will probably cover many of the requests. That does not mean your group is finished with that particular need. If a need has already been mentioned by someone else, it does not prevent you from naming it as well.

The more that need is bathed in prayer, the better. If it had been your own need, wouldn't you be glad to hear that several people brought it up in their own prayer? The more people lift it up, the more aware God will be that many people are concerned about that issue. It will become effectual fervent prayer, the kind that avails much (James 5:16). Get your two cents in.

Not everyone has the opportunity to participate and learn from those in a prayer group. An example, such as I had, is very helpful but not necessary. You can pass through the same growth process that I did while praying by myself. For me, an organized meeting had put me on a schedule that caused me to pray on a regular basis. It also provided the additional benefit of showing me the level to which the prayer life of others had grown.

You will be putting yourself on a schedule to read your Bible. The same can be done with prayer. In both cases, you can and will start small. Once you have established good habits for both, they can be lengthened.

Principles for prayer

In all probability, well before you find yourself called to the office of a prophet, you will have solidly established your prayer life. It may be the most powerful tool in your chest. God is really asking very little of us. You can do this. Learn how to pray!

Praying in Agreement

Prayer meetings are usually carried out in one of two ways. In the first, the group assembles, takes up prayer requests, and then breaks apart with each person finding his own place of prayer and praying individually for as many needs as he can recall. With eighteen people involved, there are eighteen individuals' prayers going up, a very powerful method of prayer.

> *How could one have chased a thousand, and two have put ten thousand to flight, unless their Rock had sold them, and the LORD had given them up?* (Deuteronomy 32:30)

This verse is alluding to the power when offered up in combination with another person. It is putting prayer on steroids and should yield even better results than an individual praying alone. When you stop to think about it, there is always prayer going on in many places, meaning that there are always many individual prayers taking place. In other words, assembling in one place but praying individually is still sending up eighteen individual prayers. I believe there is a way in which the power of the collective prayer can surpass that of eighteen individual prayers.

The second method also begins with the group taking up prayer requests. However, in this method, the group stays together as a unit and people pray out loud individually. While one person prays, everyone else listens and speaks out words of agreement. (Yes, Lord. Grant it, Lord. We receive it, Lord. Thank You, Jesus.) In this method, one person prays and seventeen agree. I believe this can be an even more powerful method of prayer. It is this type of prayer that is reflected in the above verse. I have not run the math on this, but eighteen who pray together must be even more powerful than two. Praying in agreement is very powerful indeed.

Fasting and Prayer

We have just seen one way prayer can be put on steroids. I have good news. There is another: fasting and prayer. Without going to a lengthy explanation of how fasting was often used, I plan to deal with only one aspect of it. It was for the purpose of influencing God to bring an answer to a specific or urgent need.

Moses fasted for forty days, which resulted in God listening to Moses (Deuteronomy 18–19). People fast as preparation before seeking divine guidance (Judges 20:26) or as a part of a ritual seeking divine favor. Mordecai first, then the Jewish community, and finally Queen Esther fasted in reaction to the decree for their destruction requested by wicked Haman (Esther 4).

Fasting is well known by Christian people today, but it is not practiced with any frequency. In the Old Testament, it seems to have been employed when an urgent and immediate response was badly needed from God. If that is correct, it may have been a very powerful weapon employed to deal with the most urgent situations. It was a hip-pocket tool.

Today, if I am hearing people correctly, when they employ fasting, they lean heavily on the effectiveness of the fasting itself. It is surely a valuable tool for use in influencing God. However, it is at its best when used in conjunction with prayer. The combination of prayer and fasting is similar to two putting ten thousand to flight.

The Old Testament prophets seemed to practice fasting more frequently than people today might. Why? Because they sensed the urgency of many situations far more clearly than we do. Should you become a prophet, you will begin to sense the urgency and you may be called on to fast with some regularity.

If praying in agreement puts prayer on steroids, and if fasting combined with prayer also puts prayer on steroids, can you imagine the power of fasting *while* praying in agreement? Would it put 100,000 to flight?

THE WAY IT CAN WORK TODAY

How Do You Get God to Move?

All of us are anxious to see God on the move. But you, as a budding young prophet, might be especially so. After all, since you are the prophet, won't others be in expectation of seeing things happen when you show up? Does that fact alone put you under pressure to come up with the goods? God moves exactly when you want Him to, right?

That's not the way it works. God is ready to move at all times. When we fail to see Him move, it's not that He wouldn't. It's that we have left in place some sort of blockage that prevents Him from moving. God is not the problem; that falls into our court. We are the problem. God can supply without measure, but we seem to be able to receive in only a limited measure. Big God, tiny us.

We cannot put God into a position where He is obligated to move. However, He may have just *deliberately* done that to Himself. He has made promises to us (Genesis 12:2 and 3, John 8:56, Leviticus 26:12–13, Deuteronomy 4:25, Psalm 12:1, 1 Chronicles 16:36, 2 Chronicles 7:14, Psalm 1:11–33), and we can remind him of them. He made His promises voluntarily, and He actually expects us to take advantage of them. He wants to move on our behalf. If we ask Him to do what He has already promised, He is stuck. What else can He do? He honors His promises. We have not because we ask not (James 4:2). All we have to do is ask.

Just because we are tiny, it does not automatically mean that we have no part in what takes place. We have to *ask* and we have to *believe*. That's the easy part. Getting the job done is the hard part. That's where God comes in. Tiny us does the easy part. Big God does the hard part. Seems fair to me.

Our own recognition of God's promises can be a tremendous reinforcement to us. If God has already bound Himself by His own word, when we remind Him what He has promised, we are also reminding ourselves about them. Knowing that He has made promises helps us to believe that He will honor them and move, just as He has promised.

God moves when He chooses. Our job is to be ready when it happens. However, we can and often do put up roadblocks that hinder God from pouring out His blessings on us. There are two big obstacles, both of which can be removed to make it more possible for God to actually do what he has wanted to do all along. They are doubt and unbelief. We can remove them and then replace them with belief and expectation.

The biggest deterrent to seeing God move is unbelief. We have covered this before, but I would like to review it and expand on the concept. Doubt and unbelief can actually be dealt with in both the spiritual and physical worlds. Both worlds can affect your opportunity to see God at work.

In the physical world, Jesus had been unable to perform many miracles in his hometown because of doubt. The doubt of His friends is of a spiritual nature, but it can be removed physically. The easiest way to overcome this problem is not to attempt to minister in the presence of doubt. Go someplace else!

You can physically move away from unbelief, but you can also remove the need from the presence of doubt.

> *And she said to Elijah, "What have you against me, O Man of God? You have come to me to bring my sin to remembrance and to cause the death of my son? And he said to her "Give me your son." And he took him from her arms and carried him into the upper chamber where he lodged, and laid him on his own bed. And he cried to the Lord, O Lord my God have you brought calamity even upon the widow with who I sojourn, by killing her son?" … And the life of the child came into him again.* (1 Kings 17:18–22 ESV)

Elijah, when confronted with the unbelief of even a strong believer, took the boy from her presence. He did not pray for the boy in the presence of unbelief of even his own mother. You might notice that she was not totally swallowed up in in unbelief. She had enough faith to entrust her son to the prophet. Not only that, but she was providing Elijah a place to live.

This woman had no small amount of faith. Yet she had some level of doubt that made it impossible for her to be involved in the prayer for her son. If you take the attitude "What could it hurt?" then you might find that it hurt a lot. Allowing doubt or unbelief to remain in the presence of prayer is a major hindrance.

Being Obedient May Mean Being Strong

How difficult would it be to disallow a person's own mother, a person who was very concerned about the life of her son, from being present for prayer? Only a strong stand removed unbelief at the key moment. However, it was doing so that permitted Elijah's prayer to be answered.

The woman had her doubts, but she wanted to believe. It is interesting that while her doubts remained, those doubts were no longer in the presence of the prayer. She remained on the ground floor while her son was taken upstairs to the room of Elijah. However, once her son was restored, she was able to believe. Hopefully when the next need arises, she will no longer be troubled with unbelief.

It may seem strange that the proximity of the doubt factored into the healing, but it seems to have been the case. Nearly all of us have prayed for missionaries in far-flung parts of the globe and had no doubt that our prayers were heard. If prayer can produce results when the one who prays and the need are thousands of miles apart, why is doubt no longer a factor when it is removed by only a single story in a house? Why does prayer have a far-reaching effect while doubt only hinders if it is nearby?

While doubt is a real factor, this difference nicely demonstrates the very great power of prayer and the limited hindrance of doubt. The contrast is immense. Prayer wins. The real issue is not the distance involved. It is that steps had been taken to separate the doubt from the need. Doubt was not permitted to be in the presence of belief.

The doubt of others needed to be removed. That had been dealt with in a physical way. While their doubt could have been dealt with in the same way that we will deal with the doubt of the one who is about to pray, there may not be much time to accomplish that. If we are going to pray now, the unbelief needs to be moved aside quickly.

The doubt of the one who is about to pray must *also* be removed. If your habit of daily Bible reading has been well developed and your prayer life has also grown, you may still have some level of doubt. That's normal. It must also be removed. That doubt must be dealt with at the spiritual level.

Do you recall that we showed how praise was able to push doubt aside by putting God in perspective? As we offer up praise, we are telling God how great He really is. We are recognizing His great accomplishments. We think that when we offer praise, we are giving glory to God. We are.

What we can easily overlook is that when we praise, we are also raising our own confidence in His greatness. That is partially due to what He has done in the past. When we think about the great things He has already done, it becomes easier to believe Him for the future. When we speak of His greatness, our own doubt and unbelief gradually diminish and our anticipation of what He might bring about increase. Our level of belief grows.

A time of praise should be held before going to the Lord with our requests. It will not only get the attention of God, but it will also build our own faith.

With the doubt of both others and ourselves removed, we have eliminated the greatest stumbling block to answered prayer. However, *unbelief may not be the only blockage to your prayers.* To move beyond that point, it may be necessary to take a long, hard look at your inner self. There may be things that you have overlooked and that may also need to be eliminated. Here are few of them.

> *But when you pray, go into your room and shut the door and pray to your Father who is in secret. And you Father who sees in secret will reward you.* (Matthew 6:6 ESV)

Prayer is not a matter for public display. It is between you and the Lord and may not be answered if it has been done for the purpose of showing it off before others.

> *And this is the confidence that we have toward him, that if we ask anything according his will he hears us.* (1 John 5:14 ESV; emphasis mine)

At the same time, we are instructed to pray according to the will of the Father. Do you know the scripture well enough to be confident you are asking for something that qualifies?

And whenever you stand and praying, forgive, if you have anything against anyone, so that your Father also which is in heaven may forgive you your trespasses. (Mark 11:25 ESV)

This is another big one. If you are holding on to unforgiveness, you are in trouble. It can be almost as major a stumbling block to prayer as unbelief. Your own sin will not be forgiven unless you are willing to forgive others, and *that* will prevent your prayers from being heard. It is a problem on two fronts.

There are more.

Likewise, husbands, live with your wives in an understanding way, sowing honor to the woman as the weaker vessel, since they are heirs with you of the grace of life, so that your prayers may not be hindered. (1 Peter 3:7)

Whoever closes his ear to the cry of the poor will himself call out and not be answered. (Proverbs 21:13 ESV)

If I had cherished iniquity in my heart, the Lord would not have listened, but truly God has listened, he has attended to the voice of my prayer. (Psalm 66:18 ESV)

Is it any wonder that so many prayers seem to go unanswered? Will you remember all these prerequisites? God is not expecting you to work from a laundry list to prepare yourself every time you pray. He is calling you to live a pure life in obedience to His plan for us all. You will grow in Him until you live up to His standard without needing to think about it all day long.

Unbelief and praying according to the will of the Father are matters that affect your relationship with God. They are a vertical issue, one between you and God. Unforgiveness is an issue between people. It is a horizontal issue. You are probably not surprised to hear that if your relationship with God, a vertical relationship, is a problem, your prayers may be hindered. But a damaged relationship with other people may also be a hindrance. While God wants you to have a perfect relationship with Him, He also want you to have a perfect relationship with other people. Those relationships are something of a proving ground. They bring us to maturity.

It might be easily to overlooked, but God is teaching you even as you are attempting to help someone else. Your relationships with others are also important and are part of what

God is doing in your own life. It's all about relationships, both between you and the Lord and between you and other people. It is the proper development of our relationships that bring us to Christian maturity.

God is continually working on many fronts. Do not be surprised to find that, even as you are being used to meet the needs of someone else, God is also working to make a change for the better in your own life. Just because you are being used, it does not mean you have arrived. Aren't you glad that God will use you even if you are not yet perfect?

A Final Review of Principles Covered

- God does not always speak in the same way.
- If you are called to be a prophet, it may not be your first place of service.
- Your first step should be to form a new habit of daily Bible reading.
- The key to your success is incremental growth.
- You can divide your time of Bible reading in four ways.
  1) Read the Bible completely through.
  2) Become an expert on one book.
  3) Do a thorough study on any verse you select.
  4) Use a portion of your time reading to have devotions.
- Think (or meditate) about what you have read.
- The length of your prayer will have small beginnings.
- Prayer may be the most powerful tool in your chest.
- Blockages to answered prayer must be removed.
- The importance of listening cannot be overstated.
- Prayer combined with fasting is similar to putting prayer on steroids.
- A pattern of prayer must become a part of your life.
- Developing good relationships both between you and God and between people are the road to Christian maturity.

What Does a Prophet Do? (Refrain)

He learns (about God).
He communes (with God).
He listens (to God).
He hears (from God).
He speaks (for God).

All that is necessary to move with God can be boiled down to the two most important elements for anyone, prophet or otherwise: listen intently and respond quickly. If these two principles can be mastered, you will be used mightily by the Lord.

Where Is Your Place of Ministry?

If the above sounds simple, it is. However, it may not be as simple to master as it seems. It is for that reason that your training program will more than likely last for several years. Even as you are being prepared, you will have had an important series of ministries all along the way. God does not train someone for years and all the while have them on the back burner. He uses people at all times during their Christian life. Seeing that you are being used by God will help to build your own faith and strengthen your relationship with Him.

I have spoken about incremental growth in this training. Ministry grows in somewhat the same way. You will have begun with a small ministry, possibly to a small group within your own church. As you grow, your ministry will also grow. That may not mean its size has grown. It is the impact that matters, and you may have trouble seeing that since you will only see what is ongoing around you, and where the effect of your effort ends up you may never know.

Where the Rubber Meets the Road

If you know that you are where God wants you, are you OK if someone else has a larger ministry? If you are unable to see the fruits of your

ministry, is that a problem? If you can believe in your spirit that your efforts have been honored by God, is that enough? If you are receiving no recognition for your efforts, can you live with that? All that can be tough.

Most of us work more effectively when our effort produces some level of approval and recognition. If a prophet works alone, he may receive no accolades. You will not be without reward; however, that may be deferred until you reach the pearly gates.

You may find that you have been involved in several different ministries, each of which has contributed to your own growth. Whether you will ever be called to function as a prophet is difficult to say. If you have done your best to prepare for whatever God has for you, you can rest in that.

Where Will I End Up?

Your place of ministry may require a change in your physical location. A pastor normally does not end up ministering in his own hometown. You may end up moving as well.

Should you eventually receive such a call, your background may actually become a *hindrance*. Both the Hebrew army and the Samaritan people had great confidence in Elisha. Even after he had begun to minister as a prophet, it would have taken time to build the confidence of the people. However, you may also recall that he had left the field that he was plowing and went with Elijah. He went somewhere else. If much is known about you and your past, you may have to do the same. Those from your hometown are those who know you best and they may be the very ones who question your ability to minister. See how doubt limited the effectiveness of even Jesus.

> *A prophet is not without honor, except in his hometown and among his relatives and in his own household. And he (Jesus, clarification added) could do no mighty work there, except that he laid his hands on a few sick people and healed them.* (Mark 6:4–5 ESV)

As powerful as Jesus's ministry was, He could do *no* mighty work there. *Even Jesus* had one hand tied behind His back when He was at home. Unbelief prevailed. If doubt and unbelief hindered His ministry, you should not be surprised to find that it also effects your own. To minister effectively, more than your own calling comes into play. The expectations of those to whom you minister will be affected by their own ability to believe. If they are filled with unbelief, you will be unable to bring effective ministry to them.

When we are at home, we are viewed as normal, average people. That's what we are, right? A prophet is not viewed as a normal, average person. He is viewed as being quite different from others. However, he is only an average person whom the Lord is using in a mighty way. To those who know him best, he is still the kid next door. "The kid next door threw a baseball through my window." He's just a kid.

You may best serve God not by instigating new programs or activities. You may be alone, coming into contact with those to whom you minister mostly when you are actually ministering. You may not be a part of the church potluck or Super Bowl party. Can you willingly give up the social aspects of the church?

All of us are normal, average people at best. We are used by the Lord not because we are better than someone else but because we are not. God is between a rock and a hard place. He has only average people from whom He can select His servants. God's servants are special only because they are humble and willing. They possess no special abilities of their own. If you feel that you have no abilities that God can use, you're right! You are the perfect choice. You are in the perfect place. You are the least of men. That's perfect.

In fact, those who do have special abilities might find them to be a hindrance to being used by God. He may initially empty you of them. Once your past is behind, you are ready to be used by God.

Even when that has been done, it may not be possible to leave your history behind. Those who know you best may continue to see you complete with your shortcomings, and that may make it difficult for them to see God through you. They may very well see the old you, not the new. However, it's not important to see the prophet. It's important to see God.

As was the case with Jesus, in your hometown, you may be surrounded with unbelief that is partially the result of people knowing what you are like. They may be unable to see past you and see God. Your old associates already know you can do very little on your own, and they are right. God is doing the work and the people need to see God, not you. It's very possible that you will be moved to a new town where your past is unknown and where you can be best used by God.

Your Placement

If you have stayed with me to this point, you may be serious about moving ahead with the Lord. God may call you into His service, and you will have very little control over what that calling might be like. He calls. You respond. *Respond* does not mean *negotiate*. Most often, your choice will only be yea or nay. I have known of cases in which someone actually did negotiate with God. However, more often than not, you will accept or decline the call.

Whose Ministry Is This Anyway?

When He calls, it will probably be to something specific, and that is where you lose control. Is it your ministry? Or is it the Lord's? Are you a control freak? God is in control. You are the servant. Control is one thing that will have to go. It's time to give it up. The good news is that you can do it!

The Lord is quite anxious to involve you and provide a place of ministry for you. He will begin to use you in small ways almost immediately after your conversion. The experiences that follow will enable you to be used by God in gradually increasing ways. It is common for a new Christian to wonder what his ultimate place of ministry might be. That may be a good thing. He is anxious to be used by the Lord, and his willingness will be rewarded.

However, concern over where he is going to be used is probably unnecessary. Looking well into the future will probably not reveal what God has for him initially. He is probably already being used in his first ministry. If it is small and nearby, it might be overlooked. For you, it will be no different. Look small, and look close.

People often look far ahead and compare themselves to someone who has already reached the very apex of his ministry. "Oh my, I could never be like him!" Maybe or maybe not, but he has not reached that point quickly. It has probably taken him years to get there, and it will take you years to reach a comparable point. A better comparison for you would be someone who is just a little beyond your own level right now. God is unique, and you can expect that His place for you will be a special place and it may not look like the ministry of anyone else.

Let's Take the Show on the Road

God does not have a quota of workers that He needs to fill. You will begin to minister when and only when you are ready. If the need is great, you will still need to complete your training. Are you ready? If so, it's time to move out.

Many will become involved in established ministries and give very little thought as to where they might best be used. Nearly always, existing ministries are in need of additional help and will be anxious to have you become involved. However, God is full of new ideas. If you seek God's face diligently about this, you might find yourself launching a brand-new ministry. God may address a need that you might never have realized exists. If you are a little adventurous, there might be something very special awaiting you.

If you are ever actually called to the ministry of a prophet, it may be later in your life and you may find that you have been in different places of service at different times. All of this may take place while you continue to grow with each stopping place making a contribution to your preparation for your ultimate ministry. Your ministry may change several times over the course of your life. Growth, all along the way, will contribute to your preparation to become a prophet.

Our biblical examples have the one called to the office of prophet entering special preparation for that and that alone immediately upon his calling. I believe the differences between the culture of biblical times and that of today will cause one to have the series of ministries that I have suggested. God will probably not immediately lead you to an isolated cave for your training. While you may receive much of your training around other students, yours will be different enough that separation may eventually become necessary.

Growth is necessarily the byword here. My church has a program for boys that emphasizes the four ways a boy grows: spiritually, mentally, physically, and socially. While that thinking is targeted to boys, I believe all of us should continue to grow (in three of them) for our entire lives.

In my own case, I am no longer a boy. My physical growth stopped about sixty-five years ago. By that, I mean vertical growth. Horizontal growth, however, has been an entirely different matter. That has continued unabated for these intervening sixty-five years. If advances in the horizontal area can be counted as a good thing, my growth has been exponential.

Our physical growth requires the continuous input of food. Spiritual growth also require requires continuous input. However spiritual growth responds to the amount of input a far better way. We do not become overweight! The potential for spiritual growth has a much more positive end. Nevertheless, as we grow spiritually, we become less concerned with things of the world. They will diminish in importance.

Wherever and whatever your greatest ministry becomes, if you have done your part in preparing to be used, you can rest easy. Your reward awaits. You may not be taken up in a whirlwind, but you will eventually go to join those who you have already influenced for eternity. Well done, good and faithful servant.

ABOUT THE AUTHOR

F. Michael Colacuori was born in 1941. World War II ended in 1945. Perhaps he might be thought of as a baby boomer. But he was a baby while things were still booming. Mike does not fit well within either the "greatest generation" or the baby boomers. He is a man without a generational matchup. While he does not fit well into a time slot, neither does he fit well into a pigeonhole that defines his thinking. While much of what he has learned has come from others, he is perfectly willing to step up and do his own thinking. "What is the next question?" the author continually asks. When we think we know the answer, nearly always there is one more question. Pushing the envelope just a little farther often brings us to the most important part of the story. It is the overlooked part that he wishes to uncover.

The author with his wife, Angie.

Printed in the United States
by Baker & Taylor Publisher Services